AMERICAN

CORPORATE

IDENTITY

2000

Edited by
David E. Carter

Cover Design
Jenette R. Williams

Production & Layout
Kristin J. Back
Alan York

Book Design
Suzanna M.W. Brown

American Corporate Identity 2000

First published 1999 by Hearst Books International
1350 Avenue of the Americas
New York, NY 10019

ISBN: 0-688-17234-2

Distributed in the U.S. and Canada by
Watson-Guptill Publications
1515 Broadway
New York, NY 10036
Tel: (800) 451-1741
          (732) 363-4511 in NJ, AK, HI
Fax: (732) 363-0338

Distributed throughout the rest of the world by
Hearst Books International
1350 Avenue of the Americas
New York, NY 10019
Fax: (212) 261-6795

Printed in Hong Kong by Everbest Printing Company through
Four Colour Imports, Louisville, Kentucky.

Table of Contents

Client
Nike Inc.
Design Firm
Mires Design
Designers
John Ball,
Deborah Hom,
Miguel Perez
Art Director
Miguel Perez

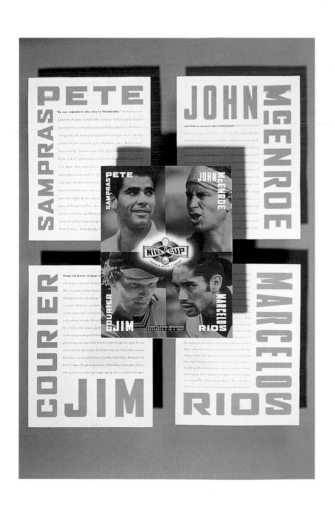

Client
  Ameren Corporation
Design Firm
  Kiku Obata & Company
Designers
  Scott Gericke, Jim Datema,
  Carole Jerome, Eleanor Safe,
  Tim Wheeler, Chris Mueller,
  Todd Mayberry

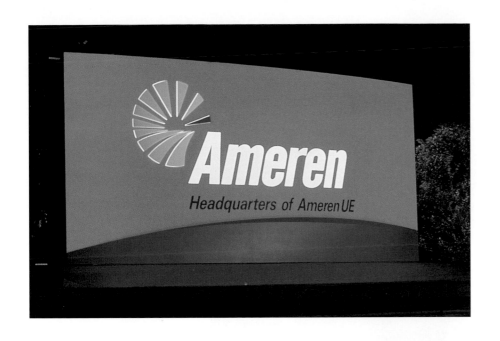

Client
Baptist Health Care
Design Firm
BrandEquity International
Designers
Anne McCuen, Todd Moxcey

Client
  Beckman Coulter, Inc.
Design Firm
  Bright/Point Zero
Designer
  Gary Hinsche

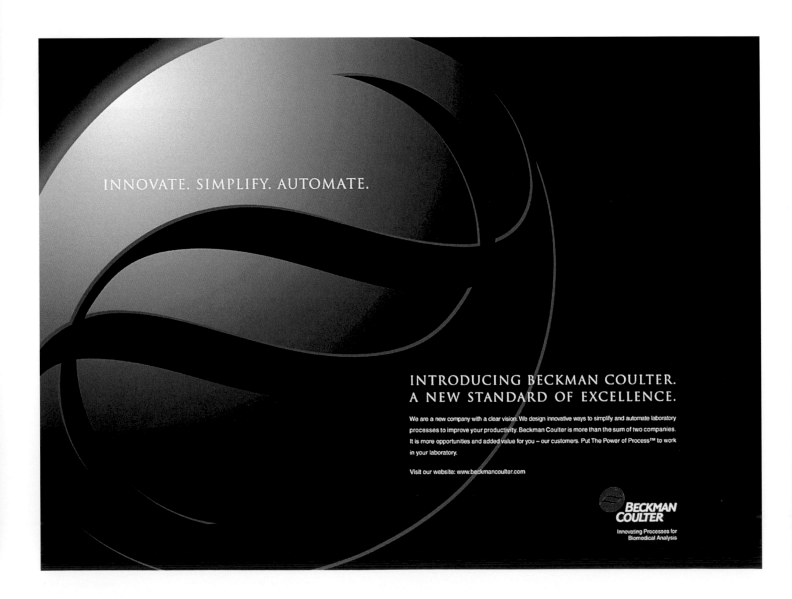

CHUGACH
HERITAGE CENTER

Client
Chugach Alaska Corporation
Design Firm
**Walsh & Associates, Inc.
and Straight Arrow Consulting**
Designer
Miriam Lisco

Kathy Cline
General Manager

Post Office Box 2388
501 Railway Avenue
Seward, Alaska 99664
Phone: (907) 224-5065
Fax: (907) 224-5075

CHUGACH
HERITAGE CENTER

Kathy Cline
General Manager

Post Office Box 2388
501 Railway Avenue
Seward, Alaska 99664
Phone: (907) 224-5065
Fax: (907) 224-5075

CHUGACH
HERITAGE CENTER

Kathy Cline
General Manager

Post Office Box 2388
501 Railway Avenue
Seward, Alaska 99664
Phone: (907) 224-5065
Fax: (907) 224-5075

CHUGACH
HERITAGE CENTER

Kathy Cline
General Manager

Post Office Box 2388
501 Railway Avenue
Seward, Alaska 99664
Phone: (907) 224-5065
Fax: (907) 224-5075

CHUGACH
HERITAGE CENTER

Client
    The Cleveland Indians
Design Firm
    Herip Associates
Designers
    Walter Herip, John Menter

Client
    David Lemley Design
Design Firm
    David Lemley Design
Designers
    David Lemley, Matt Peloza

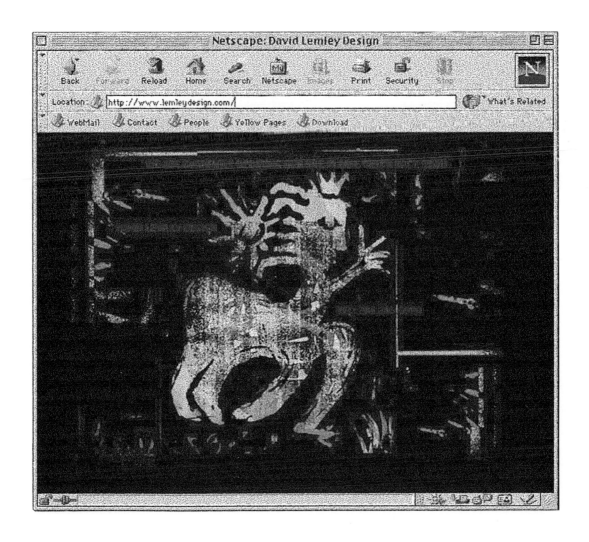

MARKETPLACE™

Client
Department Store Division of Dayton Hudson Corp.
Design Firm
Carmichael Lynch Thorburn

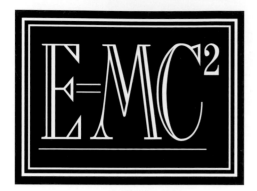

Client
  Ervin Marketing Creative Communications
Design Firm
  Ervin Marketing Creative Communications
Designer
  Mike Whitney

Client
    Finlandia Vodka Americas, Inc.
Design Firm
    Hanson Associates, Inc.
Designers
    Tobin Beck, Mary Zook

HOT SOX

Client
Hot Sox
Design Firm
Studio Morris LA/NY
Designer
Jeffrey Morris

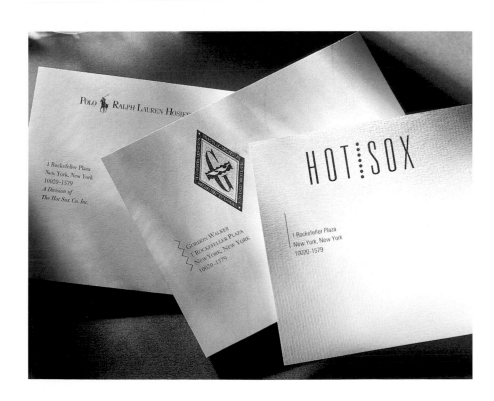

MARTHA STEWART everyday ™

Client
Kmart
Design Firm
Doyle Partners
Creative Director
Stephen Doyle

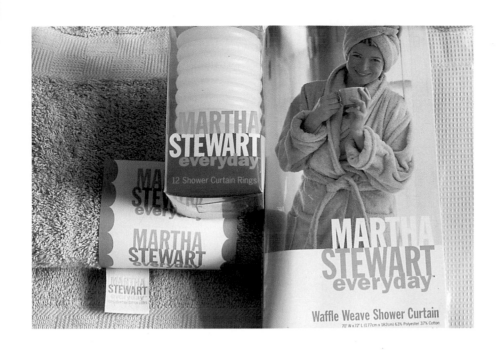

Cu novellus

Client
Novellus Systems, Inc.
Design Firm
Larsen Design Office, Inc.
Designers
Staff

BREWERY OMME GANG

Client
  Ommegang Brewery
Design Firm
  Doyle Partners
Designers
  Tom Kwepfel, Elizabeth Lee

30

31

Client
One Reel
Design Firm
David Lemley Design
Designers
David Lemley, Matt Peloza

Client
  PB&J Restaurants/
  Yahooz
Design Firm
  **EAT Advertising
  & Design, Inc.**
Designers
  Patrice Eilts-Jobe,
  DeAnne Kelly

GIFTS
OF THE
NILE

ANCIENT
EGYPTIAN
FAIENCE

Client
  Musuem of Art
  Rhode Island School of Design
Designers
  Malcolm Grear Designers

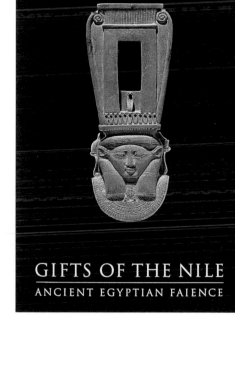

rks

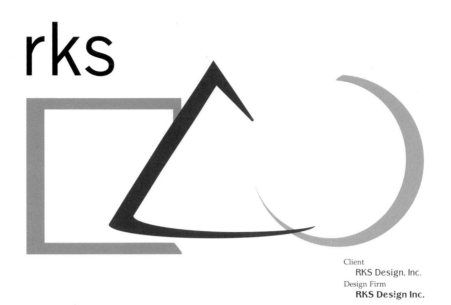

Client
RKS Design, Inc.
Design Firm
RKS Design Inc.

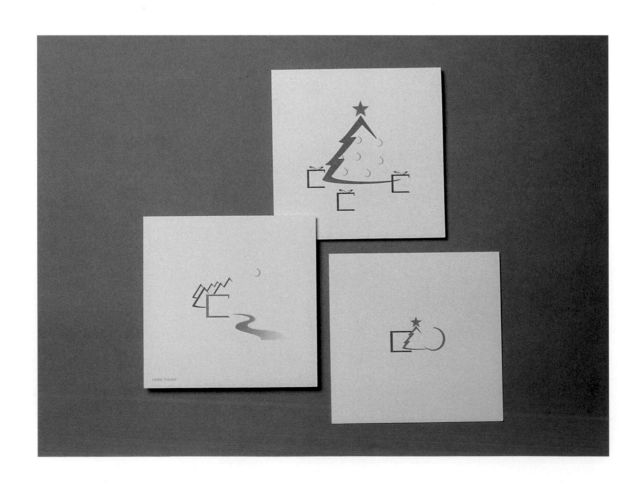

38

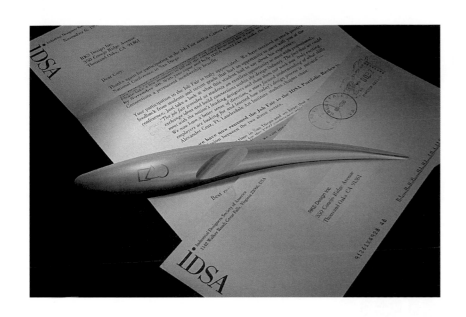

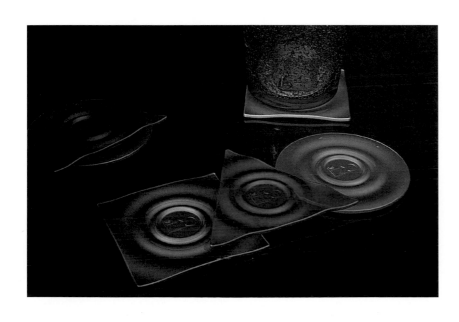

SafeGuard

Client
    SafeGuard Health Enterprises, Inc.
Design Firm
    Baker Design Associates
Designer
    Louis D'Esposito
Creative Director
    Gary Baker

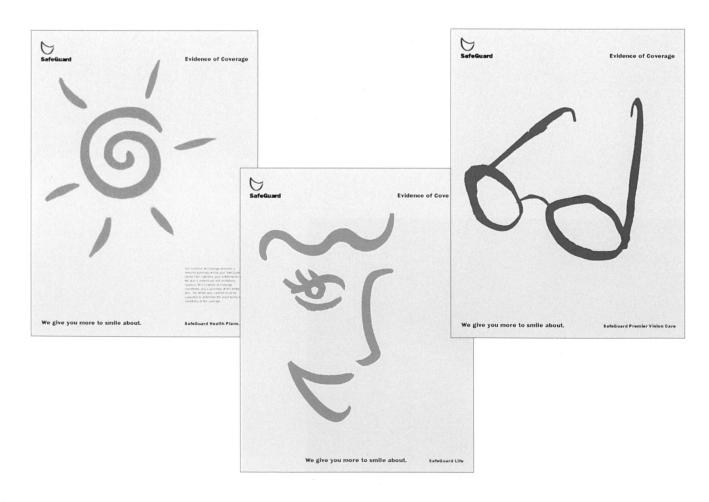

We give you more to smile about.

Broker Kit

SafeGuard

95 Enterprise
Aliso Viejo, California 92656
714.778.1005

John E. Cox
President and
Chief Operating Officer
SafeGuard Health Enterprises, Inc.

direct 714.758.4376
fax 714.758.4383
e-mail me at johnc@safeguard.net

SETTER
LEACH &
LINDSTROM

architecture
engineering
interiors

Client
   Setter Leach & Lindstrom
Design Firm
   Tilka Design
Designers
   Jane Tilka, Mark Mularz

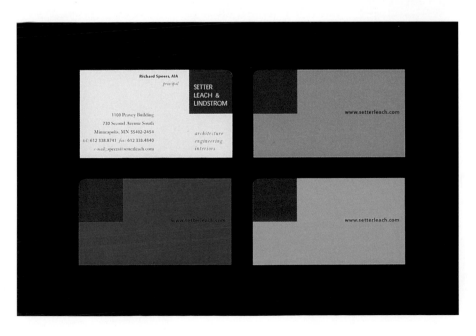

SHURGARD®

Client
Shurgard
Design Firm
Tim Girvin Design, Inc.
Designers
Aki Morino, Brian Boram

The **Speed** Art Museum

Client
The Speed Art Museum
Design Firm
Malcolm Grear Designers

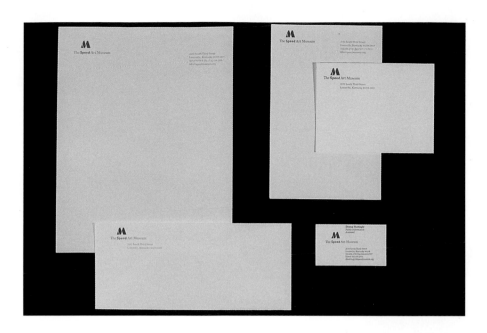

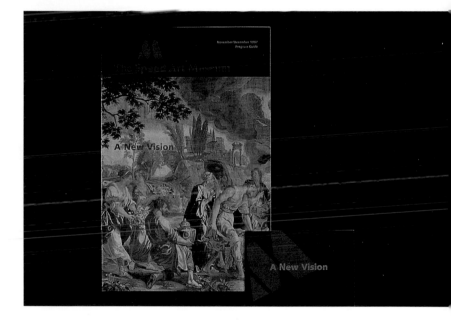

47

STACCATO'S
SOUP, STEW & CHILI BAR

Client
Stockpot Soups
Design Firm
Tim Girvin Design, Inc.
Designers
Laurie Vette, Jeff Haack

Client
  Syracuse University Athletic Department
Design Firm
  John Milligan Design
Designers
  John Milligan, Michael Milligan

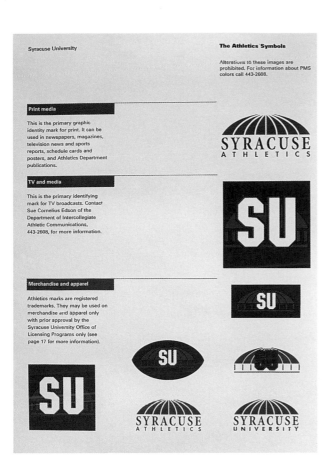

Alterations to these images are prohibited. For information about PMS colors call 443-2608.

Print media

This is the primary graphic identity mark for print. It can be used in newspapers, magazines, television news and sports reports, schedule cards and posters, and Athletics Department publications.

TV and media

This is the primary identifying mark for TV broadcasts. Contact Sue Cornelius Edson of the Department of Intercollegiate Athletic Communications, 443-2608, for more information.

Merchandise and apparel

Athletics marks are registered trademarks. They may be used on merchandise and apparel only with prior approval by the Syracuse University Office of Licensing Programs only (see page 17 for more information).

TABACALERA 1636
1636 DE ESPAÑA

Client
Tabacalera
Design Firm
Malcolm Grear Designers

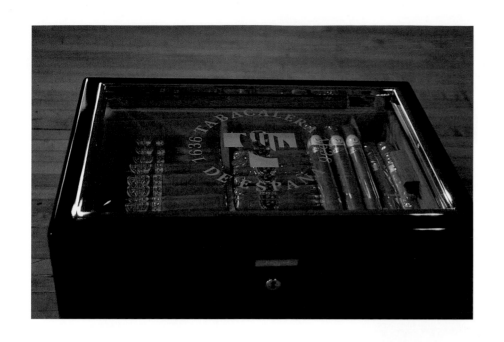

TEPLICK
LASER SURGERY CENTERS

Client
   Teplick Laser Surgery Centers
Design Firm
   Woodson & Neuroth
Designer
   Ken Steckler

TEPLICK
LASER SURGERY CENTERS

Specializing in
Laser Vision Correction
Cosmetic Laser Surgery
Advanced Cataract Surgery

Affiliated Offices In
Albany
Astoria
Beaverton
Bend
Corvallis
Dallas
Estacada
Eugene
Forest Grove
Gresham
Hillsboro
Independence
Keizer
Lake Oswego
Lebanon
Lincoln City
McMinnville
Oregon City
Portland
St. Helens
Salem
Silverton
Sublimity
Tigard
Tillamook
Vancouver
Wilsonville
Woodburn

Corporate Office
9989 SW Nimbus
Beaverton, OR 97008

Bend Laser Center
2669 Twin Knolls Drive
Bend, OR 97701

Phone 800-422-7014
Fax 503-520-0403

Stanley B. Teplick, MD Medical Director
Scott L. Nehring, OD Optometric Director

TEPLICK
LASER SURGERY CENTERS
9989 SW Nimbus, Beaverton, OR 97008

TEPLICK
LASER SURGERY CENTERS

Stanley B. Teplick M.D.
Medical Director

Pager (888) 812-0733
e-mail teplick@europa.com

Corporate Office
9989 SW Nimbus
Beaverton, OR 97008
503-520-0800

800-422-7014

Fax 503-520-0403

www.oregonlaser.com

54

Client
  Tiger Lily
Design Firm
  Hornall Anderson Design Works
Designers
  Jack Anderson, Lisa Cerveny,
  Sonja Max, Mary Hermes

Client
    U.S. Airways
Design Firm
    Deskey Associates
Designer
    Genie King

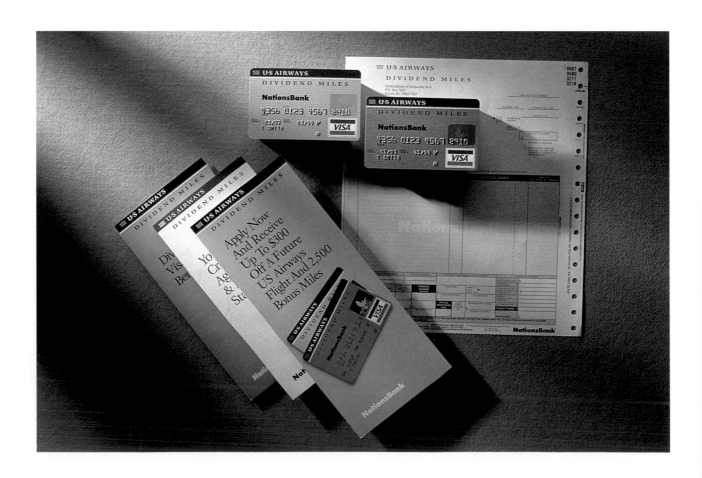

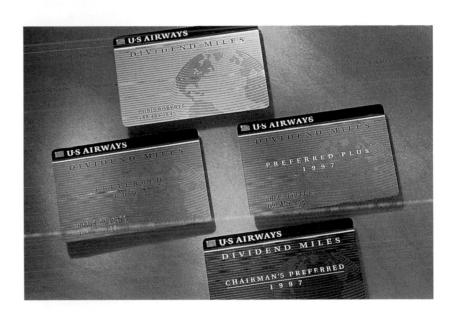

Client
Whitney/Stinger
Design Firm
Ervin Marketing Creative Communications
Designer
Jean Corea

DRINK A
WHITNEY STINGER.

There's an idea!

The Original
WHITNEY STINGER
1 1/2 ounces tequila
1 ounce sweet & sour mix
1 tablespoon lime juice
1 tablespoon lemon juice
1 teaspoon grenadine
Pinch of salt

Shake with ice and strain over ice
into an Old Fashioned glass.

Client
   X-IT Products L.L.C.
Design Firm
   Maffini & Bearce
Designer
   Philippe Maffini

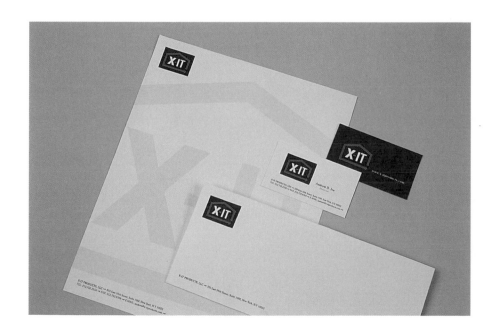

Client
   Marilyn Lysohir
Design Firm
   Delphine Keim Campbell
Designer
   Delphine Keim Campbell

Client
   Brown & Haley
Design Firm
   David Lemley Design
Designer
   David Lemley

Client
   FCS
Design Firm
   FCS
Designers
   Frank Fisher, Jackie Green

Client
   Stonewall Kitchen
Design Firm
   Leslie Evans Design Associates
Designers
   Leslie Evans, Tom Hubbard,
   Shoshannah White

Client
Montgomery Wards
Design Firm
Seasonal Specialties In House Creative
Designers
Jennifer Sheeler, Barbara J. Roth, Lisa Milan
Production
Deborah Lee, Larisa Gieneart, Rene Demel

Client
Caswell-Massey
Design Firm
David Morris Creative Inc.
Designer
Christopher Fuller

Client
JA Zenchu
Design Firm
Profile Design
Designers
Joanna Dolby, Amanda Ely,
Tony Meador, Michael Fu-Ming

Client
Saco Bay Provisioners
Design Firm
Jasper & Bridge
Designer
Alexander Bridge

Client
Delacre
Design Firm
Martini Studio
Designer
Shelley Danysh

65

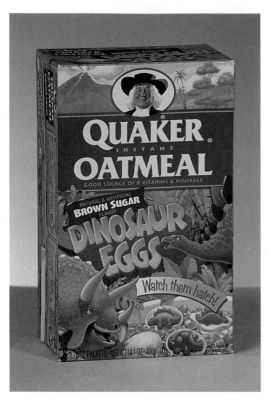

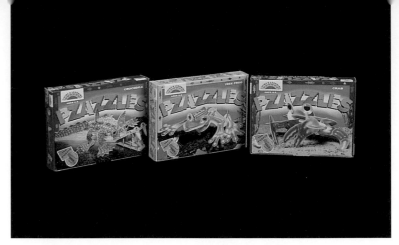

Client
    Living & Learning
Design Firm
    Hunt Weber Clark Associates
Designers
    Nancy Hunt-Weber, Gary Williams

Client
    Quaker Oats
Design Firm
    Haugaard Creative Group Inc.
Designer
    Robert Pearson

Client
    Pentech
        International
Design Firm
    **Martini
    Studio**
Designer
    Shelley Danysh

Client
    Living & Learning
Design Firm
    Hunt Weber Clark Associates
Designers
    Nancy Hunt-Weber, Leigh Krichbaum

Client
    Nestlé USA
Design Firm
    **Thompson
    Design Group**
Designers
    Kirsten Kandier,
    Davd Dzurek,
    Elizabeth Berta,
    Vernonica Denny

Client
  Upstate Farms
Design Firm
  M+P Design Group, Inc.
Designer
  Ellen Johnson

Client
  Nabisco
Design Firm
  Hans Flink Design Inc.
Designers
  Susan Kunschafl,
  Chris Notarile

Client
  Giro Sport Design
Design Firm
  **In House
  (structure by Fleetwood)**
Designer
  Maia Fong

Client
  Living & Learning
Design Firm
  Hunt Weber Clark Associates
Designers
  Nancy Hunt-Weber, Daniel Ross

Client
  Hershey Chocolate U.S.A.
Design Firm
  Zunda Design Group
Designers
  Lisa Kronmuller, Charles Zunda, Jon Voss

67

Client
A&E Television Networks
Design Firm
The Sloan Group
Art Director
Rita Arifin

Client
Rubbermaid Inc.
Design Firm
M+P Design Group, Inc.
Designer
Lisa Parenti

Client
Seasonal Specialties LLC
Design Firm
**Seasonal Specialties
In House Creative**
Designers
Jennifer Sheeler,
Barbara J. Roth, Lisa Milan
Production
Sean Zendren, Rene Demel,
Larisa Gieneart

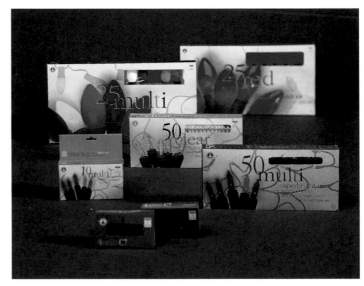

Client
Associated Students, UCLA
Design Firm
Associated Students, UCLA
Designer
Nathan Gruppman

Client
Courvoisier
Design Firm
Orbic Design Group, Ltd.
Designer
John L. Downs

Client
  SPSS Inc.
Design Firm
  **SPSS
  Creative Team**
Designers
  Deb Jansen,
  Jason Ferrara,
  Igors Irbe

Client
  Venezia/Van Noy
Design Firm
  Van Noy Group
Designers
  Amanda Park,
  Jim Van Noy

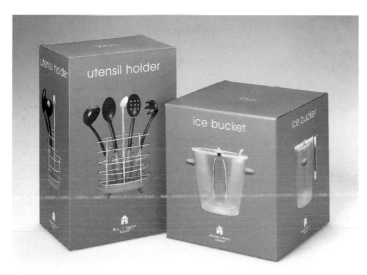

Client
  Target Stores
Design Firm
  Design Guys
Designers
  Steve Sikora,
  Gary Patch,
  Scott Thares

Client
  Rubbermaid, Inc.
Design Firm
  M+P Design Group, Inc.
Designer
  Lisa Parenti

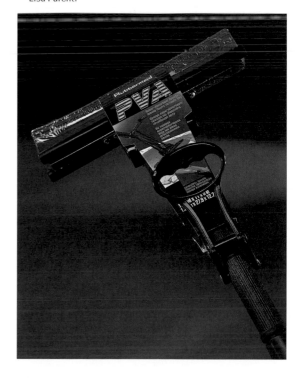

Client
  3Com
De 2sign Firm
  Studio Archetype
Designers
  Grant Peterson, Heidi Reinfeld, Patsy Hauer, Henrik Olsen

69

Client
Warner Bros. Studio Store
Design Firm
Maddocks & Company
Designers
Julia Ledyard, Catherine Cedillo

Client
McGuire Nicholas
Design Firm
Van Noy Group
Designers
Bill Murawski, Amanda Park

Client
Relationship
Enrichment Systems
Design Firm
Tusk Studios
Designer
Debra Heiser

Client
Starbucks
Design Firm
Werkhaus Design
Designer
Christina Stein

Client
Remington
Design Firm
Maddocks & Company
Designers
Julia Ledyard,
Catherine Cedillo

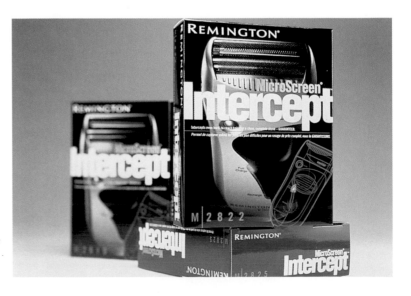

Client
   Prestone Products Corp.
Design Firm
   HMSDesign, Inc.
Designers
   Paul Beichert, Mary Ellen Butkus

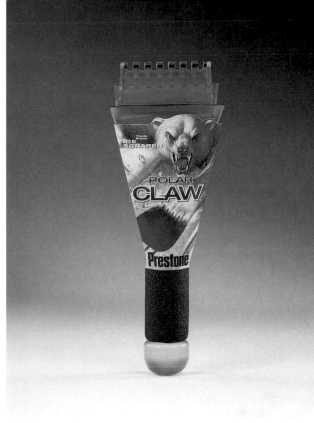

Client
   Prestone Products Corp.
Design Firm
   HMSDesign, Inc.
Designer
   Mary Ellen Butkus

Client
   Prestone Products Corp.
Design Firm
   HMSDesign, Inc.
Designers
   Mary Ellen Butkus, Kim Kelse

Client
   In-Sink-Erator International
Design Firm
   Design North, Inc.
Designers
   Mark Topczewski,
   Gwen Granzow

71

Client
The Gillette Co.
Design Firm
Phillips Design Group
Designer
Alison Goudreault

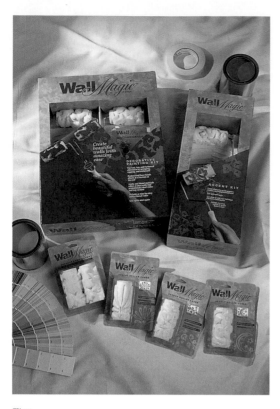

Client
Wagner
Design Firm
Hedstrom/Blessing
Designer
Pam Goebel

Client
The Limited
Design Firm
Maddocks & Company
Designers
Julia Ledyard,
Stephanie Valchar, Susan Merill

Client
InGEAR Corporation
Design Firm
**Visual
Marketing Assoc.**
Designer
Jason Selke

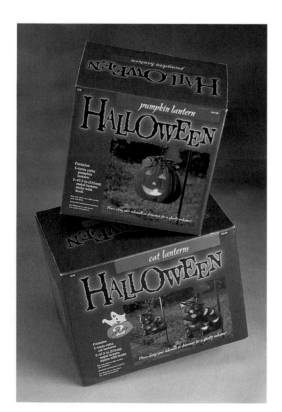

Client
Target Stores
Design Firm
Hedstrom/Blessing
Designer
Mike Goebel

Client
    Master Lock Company
Design Firm
    Design North, Inc.
Designers
    Eric Timm, Gwen Granzow

Client
    CUBE Advertising
    & Design
Design Firm
    **CUBE Advertising
    & Design**
Designer
    David Chiow

Client
    Target
Design Firm
    Hillis Mackey & Company
Designer
    Lisa Hagman

Client
    The Scotts Company
Design Firm
    Interbrand Gerstman + Meyers
Designers
    Rafael Feliciano, Frank Castaldi

Client
    Photodisc Inc.
Design Firm
    **Photodisc
    Creative Services**
Designer
    Kelly Kyer

73

Client
   Bath & Body Works
Design Firm
   Maddocks & Company
Designers
   Julia Ledyard, Nok Rumpharwan,
   Catherine Cedillo

Client
   Barbara's Bakery
Design Firm
   Gauger & Silva
Designer
   Robert Ankers

Client
   Land O' Lakes
Design Firm
   Hedstrom/Blessing
Designer
   Mike Goebel

Client
   Warner Bros. Studio Store
Design Firm
   Maddocks & Company
Designers
   Julia Ledyard, Catherine Cedillo,
   Amy Hershman, Martin Ledyard

Client
  Naturade
Design Firm
  Interbrand Gerstman + Meyers
Designers
  Chris Sanders, Mitch Gottlieb

Client
  Mead Johnson
Design Firm
  Interbrand Gerstman + Meyers
Designers
  Chris Sanders, Sabra Waxman

Client
  Playtex Products
Design Firm
  Zunda Design Group
Designers
  Paul LaPlaca, Charles Zunda, Todd Nickel

Client
  Playtex Products
Design Firm
  Zunda Design Group
Designers
  Paul LaPlaca,
  Charles Zunda, Jon Voss

75

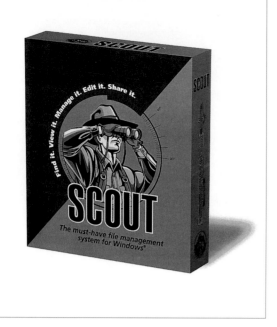

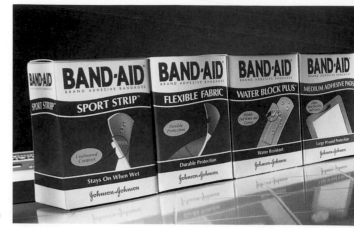

Client
Johnson
& Johnson
Design Firm
Interbrand Gerstman + Meyers
Designers
Interbrand Gerstman + Meyers Designers

Client
Thinkstream
Design Firm
Leopard Communications
Designers
Brendan Hemp,
Justin Dominguez

Client
Cirrus Logic
Design Firm
**Business
Graphics Group**
Designers
Cam Roberson,
Layne Imada

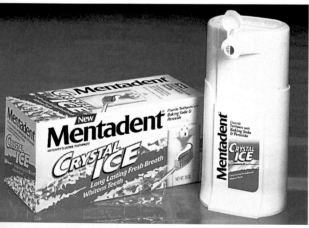

Client
Unilever HPC
Design Firm
Hans Flink Design Inc.
Designers
Mark Krukonis, Chang Mei Lin, Mike Troian

Client
The Procter &
Gamble Company
Design Firm
**Interbrand
Gerstman +Meyers**
Designers
Chris Sanders,
Michael Endy

Client
Hilton
Design Firm
Schafer
Designer
Lisa Sallwasser

Client
Professional Products of Kansas
Design Firm
Creative Visions™
Designers
Cindy Weaver, Vern Weaver

Client
Colgate Palmolive Co.
Design Firm
Hans Flink Design Inc.
Designers
Mark Krukonis, Susan Kunschaft

Client
Robinson Knife Company
Design Firm
Michael Orr + Associates, Inc.
Designers
Michael R. Orr, Thomas Freeland

Client
Unilever HPC
Design Firm
Hans Flink Design Inc.
Designers
Susan Kunschaft, Chang Mei Lin

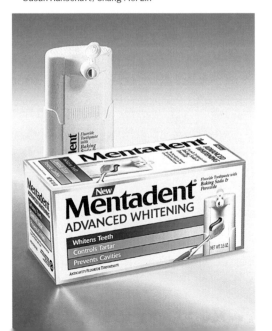

Client
  Solaris
Design Firm
  Addis Group
Designers
  David Leong, Justin Oberbauer,
  Anne Yanagi, Rosemarie Ellis

Client
  Optiva
Design Firm
  Tim Girvin Design, Inc.
Designer
  Chris Spivey

Client
  Solaris
Design Firm
  Addis Group
Designers
  David Leong,
  Justin Oberbauer,
  Paul Dorian

Client
  Boericke & Tafel
Design Firm
  Gauger & Silva
Designers
  Robert Ankers, Amy Zinsmeyer

Client
  Dial Corporation
Design Firm
  Fisher Design
Designers
  Richard Deardorff, Peter Sexton

Client
    Dial Corporation
Design Firm
    Fisher Design, Inc.
Designers
    Peter Sexton, Eric Hebert

Client
    University Games
Design Firm
    Hunt Weber Clark
Designers
    Nancy Hunt-Weber, Daniel Ross

Client
    The San Francisco Music Box Company
Design Firm
    Shields Design
Designer
    Stephanie Wong

Client
    Angelo Brothers Company
Design Firm
    Deskey Associates
Designer
    Genie King

Client
    The Scotts Company
Design Firm
    Fisher Design, Inc.
Designer
    Richard Deardorff

79

Client
Prestone Products Corp.
Design Firm
HMSDesign, Inc.
Designer
Rebecca Daw

Client
Menards
Design Firm
**Seasonal Specialties
In House Creative**
Designers
Jennifer Sheeler,
Barbara J. Roth

Client
HDS Storage Products
Design Firm
HDS Marcomm
Designer
Kim Ocumen

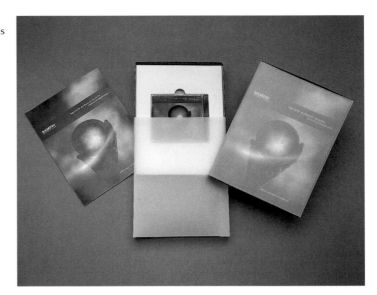

Client
Green Field Paper Company
Design Firm
Mires Design
Designers
José A. Serrano, Miguel Perez
Illustrator
Dan Thoner
Art Director
José A. Serrano

Client
Target
Design Firm
Frink Semmer

Client
  Timeworks Incorporated
Design Firm
  Kowalski Designworks, Inc.
Designer
  Krysten Bonzelet

Client
  Sherwin-Williams
Design Firm
  Interbrand Gerstman + Meyers
Designer
  Mitch Gottlieb

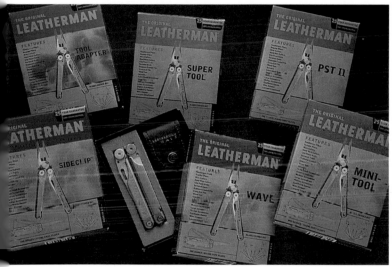

Client
  Leatherman Tool Group
Design Firm
  Hornall Anderson Design Works
Designers
  Jack Anderson, Lisa Cerveny,
  David Bates, Alan Florsheim

Client
  Taylor Made Golf
Design Firm
  **Laura Coe
  Design Associates**
Designers
  Laura Coe Wright,
  Ryoichi Yotsumoto

Client
  Pamida Stores
Design Firm
  Seasonal Specialties In House Creative
Designers
  Lisa Milan, Jennifer Sheeler
Production
  Lisa Milan, Clay Schotzko

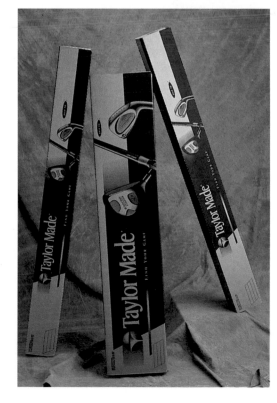

81

Client
  Supre
Design Firm
  Swieter Design U.S.
Designers
  Mark Ford, John Swieter

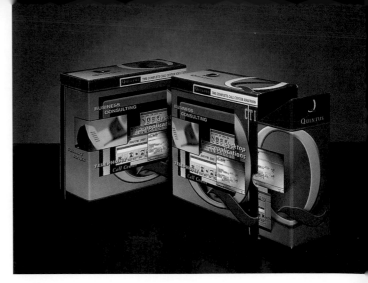

Client
  Quintus
Design Firm
  **Balderman
  Creative Services**
Designer
  Bobbi Balderman

Client
  Shopko Stores
Design Firm
  Seasonal Specialties In House Creative
Designers
  Lisa Milan, Jennifer Sheeler, Barbara J. Roth

Client
  Bath & Body Works
Design Firm
  Design Guys
Designer
  Jay Theige

Client
  Ricci's Salon
Design Firm
  Connolly & Connolly, Inc.
Designer
  Joe Connolly

Client
Dial
Corporation
Design Firm
**Fisher
Design, Inc.**
Designers
Lynne Chrapliwy,
Peter Sexton,
Eric Hebert

Client
Joico
Design Firm
**Maddocks
& Company**
Designers
Mary Scott,
Winnie Li,
Paul Farris,
Ann Utley-Moores

Client
Viacom
Consumer Products
Design Firm
30sixty design, inc.
Designers
Pär Larssen,
Rickard Olsson,
Peggy Martin

Client
Unilever HPC
Design Firm
Hans Flink Design Inc.
Designers
Chang Mei Lin, Susan Kunschaft

Client
Le Mar
Design Firm
Pedersen Gesk
Designer
Rony Zibara

Client
   Westwood Studios
Design Firm
   Creative Dynamics Inc.
Designer
   Eddie Roberts

Client
   Gaetano Specialties,Ltd.
Design Firm
   Van Noy Group
Designer
   Bill Murawski

Client
   Canandaigua Wine Co.
Design Firm
   M+P Design Group, Inc.
Designers
   Stephen Palozzi, Dennis DeSilva

Client
   Encyclopaedia
   Britannica
Design Firm
   **Tim Girvin
   Design, Inc.**
Designers
   Kim Edberg,
   Thomas Lehman

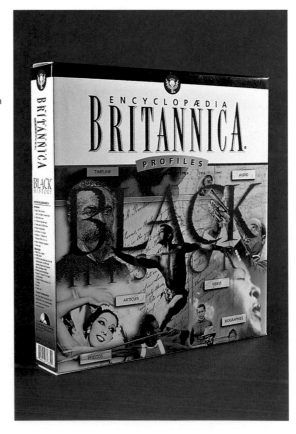

Client
  Photodisc Inc.
Design Firm
  Photodisc Creative Services
Designer
  Kelly Kyer

Client
  Waterbrook Winery
Design Firm
  Giordano Kearfott Design
Designers
  Susan Giordano, Lee Ater,
  Mike McIvor, Diane Christensen

Client
  William Grant & Sons
Design Firm
  **Bailey Design
  Group, Inc.**
Designer
  Paula Elrod

Client
  Valve
Design Firm
  The Leonhardt Group
Designers
  Jan Cannell,
  Ray Ueno, Jan King

Client
    Donatos Pizza
Design Firm
    Chude Gerdeman, Inc.
Designer
    Adam Limbach

Client
    Ben & Jerry's
Design Firm
    Zunda Design Group
Designers
    Ben Nooney, Mary Lou Kelley,
    Paul Newman, Charles Zunda

Client
    Weight Watchers
Design Firm
    The Blondo Group
Designers
    Blondo Team

Client
    Jenkins Foods
Design Firm
    FCS
Designers
    Frank Fisher, Dennis Halezyty

Client
    Coca-Cola Southwest
Design Firm
    Creative Link Studio, Inc.
Designers
    Kevin La Rue, Kyle Derr,
    Mark Broderick

Client
General Mills
Design Firm
Hillis Mackey & Company
Designer
Randy Szarzynski

Client
Kraft Foods
Design Firm
The Blondo Group
Designers
Blondo Team

Client
General Mills—Betty Crocker
Design Firm
Thompson Design Group
Designer
Dave Dzurek

Client
Alberto-Culver USA
Design Firm
The Blondo Group
Designers
Blondo Team

Client
Pepperidge Farms
Design Firm
Martini Studio
Designer
Shelley Danysh

Client
   Land O' Lakes
Design Firm
   Hedstrom/Blessing
Designer
   Brent Swanson

Client
   Just Born Inc.
Design Firm
   Bailey Design Group, Inc.
Designers
   Steve Perry, Amy Grove Bigham

Client
   University Games
Design Firm
   Hunt Weber Clark Associates
Designers
   Nancy Hunt-Weber, Daniel Ross

Client
   David Leong
Design Firm
   Addis Group
Designers
   David Leong, Robin Maclean

Client
   Cloud Nine
Design Firm
   Hornall Anderson Design Works
Designers
   Jack Anderson, Jana Nishi,
   Heidi Favour, David Bates,
   Mary Hermes, Taro Sakita, Virginia Le

Client
  Target Stores
Design Firm
  Hedstrom/Blessing
Designer
  Mike Goebel

Client
  Taylor Made Golf
Design Firm
  Laura Coe Design Associates
Designers
  Laura Coe Wright, Denise Heisly

Client
  Hasbro Toys
Design Firm
  Fisher Design
Designer
  Jeff Meyers, Sr.

Client
  Target Stores
Design Firm
  Hedstrom/Blessing
Designer
  Wendy LaBreche

Client
  Uniquely Arizona
Design Firm
  Morgan & CO.

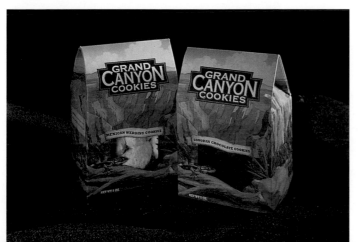

Client
Pioneer Electronics (USA) Inc.
Design Firm
Jensen Design Associates
Designers
David Jensen, Bob Rayburn, Jerome Calleja

Client
Fox Sports
Television
Design Firm
Taylor Design
Designers
Daniel Taylor, Jennifer Whitaker

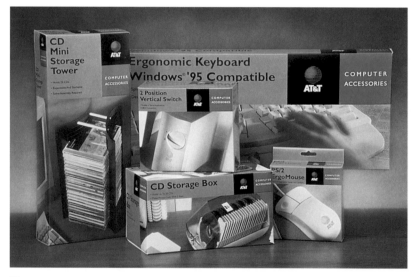

Client
Eastman Kodak Company
Design Firm
Forward Design Inc.
Designer
Tim Blazejewski

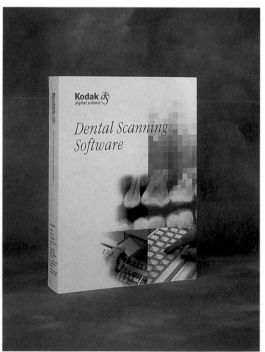

Client
Gemini Industries
Design Firm
LMS Design
Designer
Richard Shear

Client
Motherlode Band
Design Firm
The Weller Institute
Designer
Don Weller

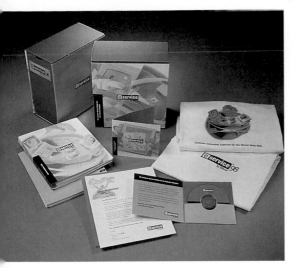

Client
  Silknet
Design Firm
  Luma Design
Designer
  Lisa Thayer

Client
  Laser Publishing Group
Design Firm
  Imtech Communications
Designer
  Robert Keng

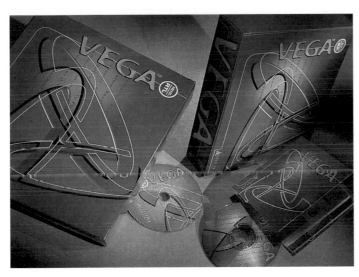

Client
  Paradigm
Design Firm
  David Carter Design Assoc.
Designer
  Tien Pham
Creative Director
  Lori B. Wilson

Client
  Berkeley Systems
Design Firm
  Addis Group
Designers
  James Eli, Rick Atwood, Bob Hullinger

Client
  3M Optical Systems Division
Design Firm
  Hedstrom/Blessing
Designer
  Wendy LaBreche

Client
Infinity Industries Inc.
Design Firm
66 communication inc.
Designers
Chin-Chih Yang, Jessica Lin

Client
Valio
Design Firm
Interbrand Gerstman+Meyers
Designers
Interbrand Gerstman+Meyers Designers

Client
Kaytee Products, Inc.
Design Firm
Design North, Inc.
Designers
Gwen Granzow,
Steve Stocker,
Jackie Langenecker

Client
Paul Walter
Design Firm
Thomas Hillman Design
Designer
Thomas Hillman

Client
Char Crust, Inc.
Design Firm
Murrie Lienhart Rysner
Designer
Linda Voll

92

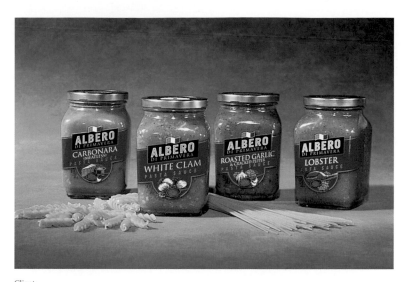

Client
Spring Tree
Design Firm
Kollberg/Johnson
Designers
Michael Carr, Gary Kollberg

Client
Gloria's Kitchen
Design Firm
Hunt Weber Clark Associates
Designers
Nancy Hunt Weber, Christine Chung

Client
H.E.B.
Design Firm
Murrie Lienhart Rysner
Designer
Linda Voll

Client
Laredo and Lefty's
Design Firm
Hillis Mackey & Company
Designer
Randy Szarzynski

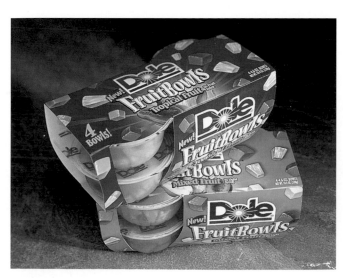

Client
Dole Packaged Foods
Design Firm
Addis Group
Designers
Ariel Villasol, Joanne Hom

Client
    Canandaigua
Design Firm
    **Forward
    Design Inc.**
Designer
    Daphne Stofer

Client
    Hiram Walker
Design Firm
    Van Noy Group
Designer
    Amanda Park

Client
    Seagram's
Design Firm
    Port Miolla Assoc.
Designer
    Robert Swan

Client
    August Schell Brewing Co.
Design Firm
    Compass Design
Designers
    Mitchell Lindgren,
    Tom Arthur, Rich McGowen

Client
    Canandaigua Wine
Design Firm
    Forward Design Inc.
Designers
    Forward Design

Client
  August Schell Brewing Co.
Design Firm
  Compass Design
Designers
  Mitchell Lindgren, Tom Arthur, Rich McGowen

Client
  August Schell Brewing Co.
Design Firm
  Compass Design
Designers
  Mitchell Lindgren,
  Tom Arthur, Rich McGowen

Client
  Vegas Valley Brewery
Design Firm
  Creative Dynamics
Designers
  Eddie Roberts, John Massé, Casey Corcoran

Client
  Gaetano Specialties, Ltd
Design Firm
  Van Noy Group
Designers
  Bill Murawski, Amanda Park

Client
  Seagram's
Design Firm
  Port Miolla Assoc.
Designer
  Robert Swan

Client
Target
Design Firm
Compass Design
Designers
Mitchell Lindgren,
Tom Arthur, Rich McGowen

Client
CBI Laboratories
Design Firm
Maddocks & Company
Designers
Mary Scott, Julia Ledyard

Client
Victoria's Secret
Design Firm
Desgrippes Gobé
Designers
Susan Hopper,
Patricia Leunis

Client
Colgate-Palmolive
Design Firm
Kollberg/Johnson
Designer
Penny Johnson

Client
Gianna Rose
Design Firm
**Sayles
Graphic Design**
Designer
John Sayles

96

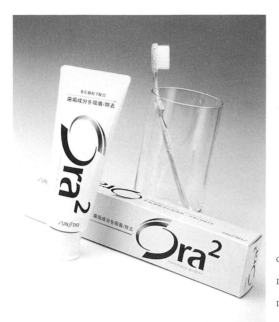

Client
Murad Inc.
Design Firm
Maddocks & Company
Designers
Mary Scott, Catherine Cedillo,
Paul Farris, Mary Cay Walp

Client
Sunstar, Inc.
Design Firm
Desgrippes Gobé
Designers
Susan Berson,
Deirdre Tighe

Client
CBI Laboratories
Design Firm
Desgrippes Gobé
Designer
Susan Berson

Client
Target
Design Firm
Compass Design
Designers
Mitchell Lindgren,
Tom Arthur,
Rich McGowen

Client
Versace
Design Firm
Desgrippes Gobé

97

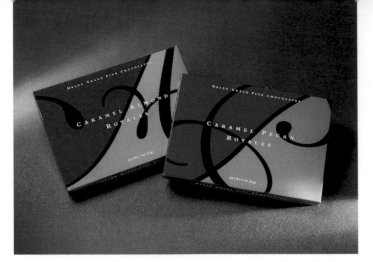

Client
  Helen Grace Fine Chocolates
Design Firm
  30sixty design, inc.
Designers
  Pär Larsson, Teekaryn Potivas,
  Peggy Martin

Client
  Con Agra
Design Firm
  Hillis Mackey & Company
Designer
  Terri Gray

Client
  Interocean Seafoods Co.
Design Firm
  **Faine-Oller
  Productions, Inc.**
Designers
  Catherine Oller

Client
  Mayer Bros.
Design Firm
  M+P Design Group, Inc.
Designer
  Lisa Parenti

Client
  Jamaican Gourmet Coffee Company
Design Firm
  **Kevin Hall
  Design**
Designer
  Kevin Hall

Client
Cafe Au Lait
Design Firm
30sixty design, inc.
Designer
Pår Larsson

Client
Lea & Perrins
Design Firm
Wallace/Church
Designers
Stan Church, Paula Patricola, Wendy Church

Client
Imagine Foods
Design Firm
Gauger & Silva
Designer
Isabelle Laporte

Client
JTM Provisions, Inc.
Design Firm
Fisher Design, Inc.
Designers
Peter Sexton,
Maria Ramstetter

Client
Lipton
Design Firm
Port Miolla Assoc.
Designer
Rob Swan

Client
Mazola
Design Firm
Wallace/Church
Designers
Stan Church, Jae Cuticone, Wendy Church

Client
Morey's Seafood
Design Firm
Hillis Mackey & Company
Designer
Terri Gray

Client
Barbara's Bakery
Design Firm
Gauger & Silva
Designers
Isabelle Laporte,
Laura Levy

Client
Yves Veggie Cuisine
Design Firm
Hornall Anderson Design Works
Designers
John Hornall, Debra McCloskey,
Heidi Favour, Michael Brugman,
Jana Wilson Esser

Client
Byblos
Design Firm
Adkins/Balchunas
Designer
Matthew Fernberger

Client
  Ocean Beauty Seafood
Design Firm
  Faine-Oller Productions, Inc.
Designers
  Catherine Oller, Barbara Faine

Client
  BC—USA
Design Firm
  LMS Design
Designer
  Richard Shear

Client
  Swift Premium
Design Firm
  Haugaard Creative Group Inc.
Designer
  José Parado

Client
  Aunt Gussie's Cookies & Crackers
Design Firm
  Compass Design
Designers
  Tom Arthur, Mitchell Lindgren, Rich McGowen

Client
  Lipton
Design Firm
  Port Miolla Assoc.
Designer
  Paul Port

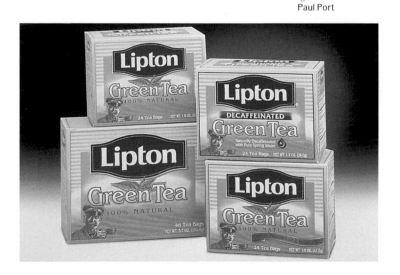

Client
  Murad Inc.
Design Firm
  Maddocks & Company
Designers
  Mary Scott, Catherine Cedillo,
  Paul Farris, Mary Cay Walp

Client
  Bausch & Lomb
Design Firm
  Forward Design
Designer
  Daphne Stofer

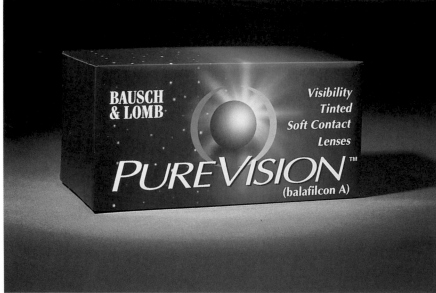

Client
  Gianna Rose
Design Firm
  Sayles Graphic Design
Designer
  John Sayles

Client
  Gillette
Design Firm
  Wallace/Church
Designers
  Stan Church, David Minkley

Client
  Johnson & Johnson
Design Firm
  Bailey Design Group, Inc.
Designer
  Steve Perry

Client
  St. John
Design Firm
  Maddocks & Company
Designers
  Mary Scott, Ann Utley-Moores, Julia Ledyard

Client
  Target
Design Firm
  Compass Design
Designer
  Tom Arthur,
  Mitchell Lindgren,
  Rich McGowen

Client
  The Gillette Co.
Design Firm
  Phillips Design Group
Designer
  Alison Goudreault

Client
  The Maxell Corporation of America
Design Firm
  Bailey Design Group, Inc.
Designer
  Gary LaCroix

Client
  Liz Claiborne
Design Firms
  **Parham Santana,
  Liz Claiborne**
Designer
  Ann Sappenfield
Art Directors
  Lori Reinig, Barrie Glabman
Creative Directors
  Maruchi Santana, Lynda Greenblatt

Client
  Duck Head Apparel Co.
Design Firm
  Desgrippes Gobe
Designers
  Lori Yi, Tom Davidson, Joy Liu

Client
  General Cigar
Design Firm
  LMS Design
Designers
  Richard Shear, Alex Williams

Client
    Discovery Communications Inc.
Design Firm
    Discovery Design Group
Designers
    Mike Zizza, Lynne Heiser, Holli Rathman
Art Director
    Janet Daniel

Client
    Polo Ralph Lauren
Design Firm
    Parham Santana Inc.
Designer
    Dave Wang
Art Director
    Lori Reinig
Creative Director
    Maruchi Santana

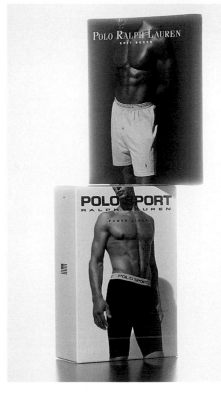

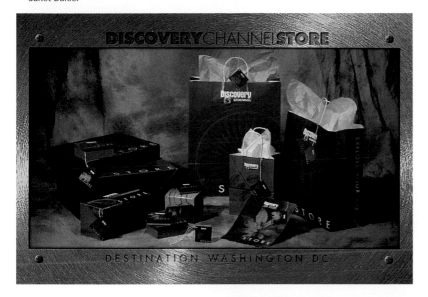

Client
    American Cancer Society
Design Firm
    Sayles Graphic Design
Designer
    John Sayles

Client
    Andover Powerflex
Design Firm
    BrandEquity International
Designer
    Bill Kenney

Client
    Pennsylvania
    Fashions
Design Firm
    JGA, Inc.
Designers
    Tony Camilletti,
    Brian Eastman,
    Mike Farris

Client
    Friendly Ice Cream Corporation
Design Firm
    Luis R. Lee & Associates
Designers
    Luis R. Lee, Heather VanLoan

Client
    Keebler Company
Design Firm
    Cassata & Associates
Designers
    Jim Wolfe, Todd Palminteri

Client
    Greenfield's
Design Firm
    Martini Studio
Designer
    Shelly Danysh

Client
    Golden Valley
    Microwave Foods
Design Firm
    Hillis Mackey & Company
Designer
    Jeff Hillis

Client
  Vt. Pure
Design Firm
  The Imaginaton Company
Designers
  Bronwen Battaglia, Kieran McCabe

Client
  UDV North America
Design Firm
  Bailey Design Group, Inc.
Designers
  David Fiedler,
  Wendy Seldomridge

Client
  City Delights
Design Firm
  Van Noy Group
Designer
  Bill Murawski

Client
  Nabisco
Design Firm
  **Murrie
  Lienhart Rysner**
Designers
  Annie Donlin

Client
   Schwan's
Design Firm
   Pedersen Gesk
Designers
   Rony Zubara

Client
   San-J International, Inc.
Design Firm
   Gauger & Silva
Designer
   Lori Murphy

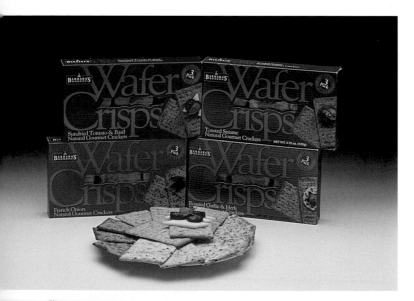

Client
   Barbara's Bakery
Design Firm
   Gauger & Silva
Designer
   Robert Ankers

Client
   Imagine Foods
Design Firm
   Gauger & Silva
Designer
   Isabelle Laporte

108

Client
  Cargill
Design Firm
  Pedersen Gesk
Designer
  Roger Remaley

Client
  Schwan's
Design Firm
  Pedersen Gesk
Designer
  Roger Remaley

Client
  Fleming
Design Firm
  Pedersen Gesk
Designer
  Rony Zubara

Client
  Bel Canto Fancy Foods Ltd.
Design Firm
  Susan Meshberg Graphic Design
Designers
  Susan Meshberg, Paul Calabro

Client
Sümer
Distributing
Design Firm
**Sayles
Graphic
Design**
Designer
John Sayles

Client
Olivet
Design Firm
Louisa Sugar Design
Designers
Louisa Sugar, Beth O'Rourke,
Donald Churchfield

Client
UDV North America
Design Firm
**Bailey's Design
Group, Inc.**
Designer
Jeff Behrenhauser

Client
Finlandia Vodka Americas, Inc.
Design Firm
Hanson Associates, Inc.
Designer
Tobin Beck

Client
G&V Company
Design Firm
Shields Design
Designer
Charles Shields

Letterheads are presented perpendicular to the
remainder of the book for larger representation.

*L*etterhead Designs

900 JEFFERSON ROAD

ROCHESTER, NEW YORK

14623

PHONE 716-272-7864

Client
Interior Focus
Design Firm
Fuller Designs, Inc.
Designer
    Doug Fuller

Client
Newbury Park Pastries
Design Firm
Forward Design Inc.
Designers
Daphne Stofer, Wendy Foster

Interior Focus, LLC
Staging Consultation for
Real Estate Professionals

2045 Beacon Place
Reston, Virginia 20191
703-860-9407
703-860-0544 /fax

Client
Odyssey International
Design Firm **Swieter Design U.S.**
Designer
John Swieter

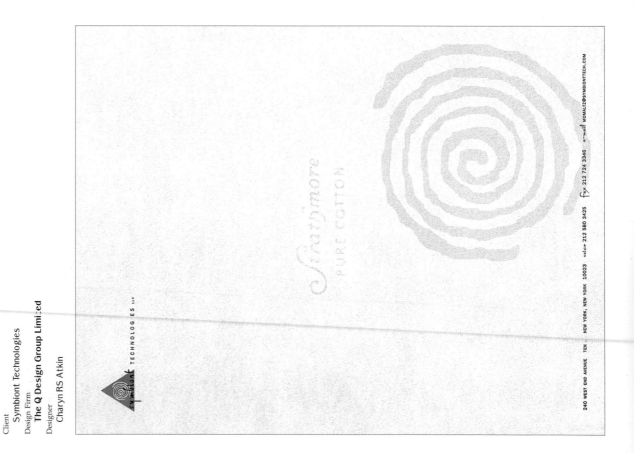

Client
Symbiont Technologies
Design Firm **The Q Design Group Limited**
Designer
Charyn RS Atkin

Client
Del Norte Neighborhood Development Corporation
Design Firm **Rassman Design**
Designers
John Rassman, Amy Rassman, Lyn D'Amato, Vicki Freeman

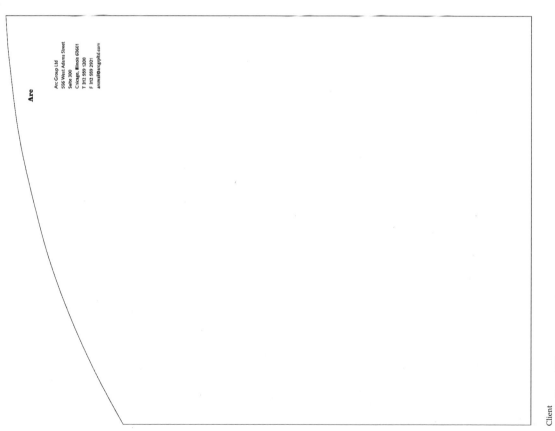

Client
Arc Group LTD
Design Firm **Arc Group LTD**
Designer
William Hafeman

Client
Mike Rabe Music Engraving
Design Firm
Design Guys
Designer
Amy Kirkpatrick

MIKE RABE MUSIC ENGRAVING

1991 Brewster Street
Saint Paul, Minnesota 55108

612.647.6803
rabex005@tc.umn.edu

Lovell&Whyte
14950 Lakeside Road
Lakeside, Michigan 49116
616 469 5900 Phone
616 469 9998 Fax

Client
Lovell & Whyte
Design Firm
Kym Abrams Design
Designer
Kym Abrams, Amy Nathan

329 10th Avenue SE
Cedar Rapids, IA 5240
TEL: 319.364.8859
FAX: 319.362.3701
http://www.strongdesign—.com
strong@fyiowa.infi.net

STRONG PRODUCTIONS INC.

Client
Strong Productions
Design Firm
Strong Productions
Designers
Brian Cox, Matt Doty

JAMES ELLIOT

Client
James Elliot Jewelers
Design Firm
Muller + Co.
Designers
John Muller, Jeff Miller

SCOTTSDALE | BORGATA

6166 NORTH SCOTTSDALE RD., #702 SCOTTSDALE, ARIZONA 85253 | 602.368.9009 | FAX 602.368.9229 | jameselliot.com

Client
EPIC
Design Firm
Crowley Webb & Associates
Designer
Dion Pender

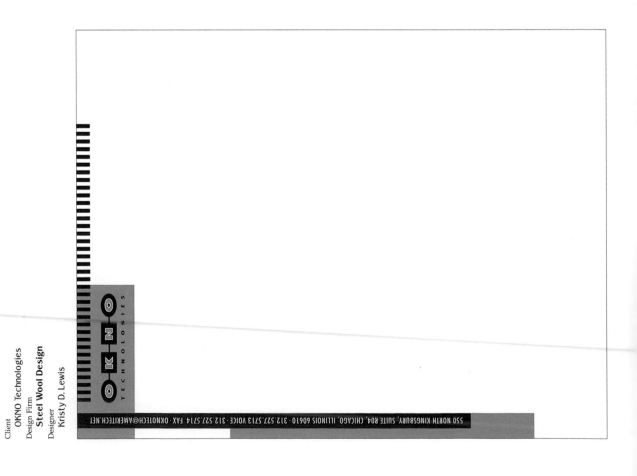

Client
OKNO Technologies
Design Firm
Steel Wool Design
Designer
Kristy D. Lewis

Southwest Jet Corporate Center
14988 North 78th Way, #220
Scottsdale, Arizona 85260

Www.i-sites.com
P 602.707.1600
F 602.707.1601

Client
Interactive Sites
Design Firm **Duke Marketing Communications**
Designers
Justin Ahrens, Chad Nelson

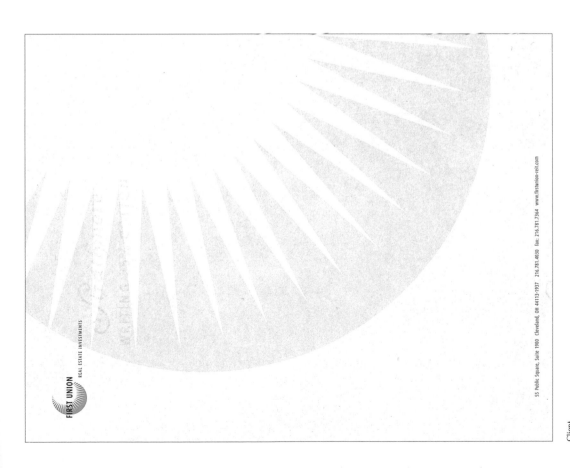

55 Public Square, Suite 1900 Cleveland, OH 44113-1937 216.781.4030 fax: 216.781.7364 www.firstunion-reit.com

Client
First Union Real Estate Investments
Design Firm **Karen Skunta & Company**
Designers
Christopher Suster, Karen A. Skunta

Graceland Cemetery and Crematorium
Trustees of the Graceland Cemetery Improvement Fund

4001 N. Clark Street Chicago, Illinois 60613 773.525.1105 Fax: 773.525.9091

5777 GRANT AVENUE CLEVELAND OHIO 44105 FAX 216.341.0534 PHONE 216.341.1000

FORTRAN PRINTING INC.

GARVER NAGY

GARVER NAGY

INTERIORS GROUP

1100 LAKE STREET

SUITE LL40

OAK PARK, IL 60301

T 708 524 4966

F 708 445 0124

Client
　Garver Nagy Interiors
Design Firm
　Nicholas Associates/Chicago
Designer
　Nick Sinadinos

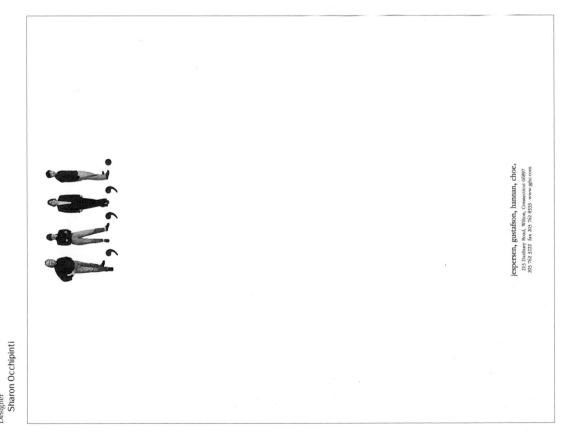

jespersen, gustafson, hannan, choe.
215 Danbury Road, Wilton, Connecticut 06897
203 762 3222 fax 203 762 8533 www.gjhc.com

Client
　J, G, H, C.
Design Firm
　JOE Advertising
Designer
　Sharon Occhipinti

119

ENGLE + MURPHY

236 East 3rd Street Suite 210 Long Beach Ca 90802 Telephone 562.983.7276 Fax 562.983.7274

Client
Engle and Murphy
Design Firm
Engle and Murphy
Designer
Alan Otto

Client
American Bankers Association
Design Firm
IconixGroup
Designer
Heide Paddock

ABAecom

A subsidiary of the AMERICAN BANKERS ASSOCIATION

Strathmore
WRITING 25% COTTON
RECYCLED

www.ABAecom.com   800•338•0626   1120 CONNECTICUT AVENUE, NW   WASHINGTON, DC 20036

Client
  Just One
Design Firm
  After Hours Creative
Designers
  After Hours Creative

Client
  Colorado's Ocean Journey
Design Firm
  Rassman Design
Designers
  John Rassman, Amy Rassman, Lyn D'Amato,
  Vicki Freeman, Gwyn Browning

121

Client
  Oxbow
Design Firm
  Rick Johnson & Company, Inc.
Designer
  Tim McGrath
Production
  Ted Slampyak

8110 LOMAS NE ALBUQUERQUE, N.M. 87110 TEL: 505.265.8996 FAX: 505.265.8997

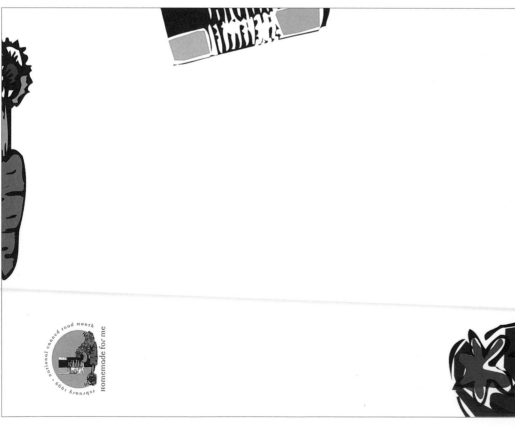

Homemade for me

canned food alliance • six ppg place • pittsburgh, pa 15222

Client
  Canned Food Alliance
Design Firm
  A to Z communications, inc.
Designer
  Vonnie Hornburg

122

UPSTREAM
BREWING
COMPANY
514 SOUTH
ELEVENTH
STREET
OMAHA
NEBRASKA
68102

Fax 402.344.0451
402.344.0200

Client
Upstream Brewing Company
Design Firm
David Day & Associates
Designer
David Day

Client
Wyse Landau Public Relations
Design Firm
Nesnadny + Schwartz
Designer
Joyce Nesnadny, Michelle Moehler

World Wide Public Relations Services

WYSE·LANDAU

25 Prospect Avenue, West, Cleveland, Ohio 44115   Fax 216-736-4403   216-696-1686

Client
GNT Audio Video Systems
Design Firm **Groft Design**
Designer
Randy Groft

Client
Brent Humphries, Photographer
Design Firm **Swieter Design U.S.**
Designer
Mark Ford

Client
New Vision Communications Corporation
Design Firm **Stark Design**

Client **Groft Design**
Design Firm **Groft Design**
Designer Randy Groft

Client
Electrical Accident Group
Design Firm
LF Banks + Associates
Designers
Lori Banks, John German

Client
Windholm Partners
Design Firm
Tollner Design Group
Designer
Christopher Canote

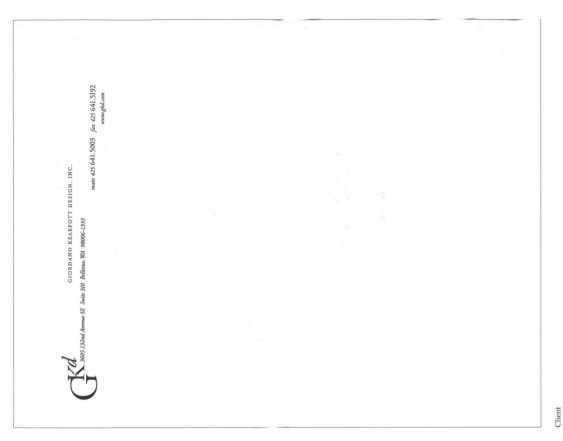

GIORDANO KEARFOTT DESIGN, INC.

3605 132nd Avenue SE Suite 310 Bellevue, WA 98006-1333

main 425 641.5003 fax 425 641.5192

www.gkd.com

Client
Giordano Kearfott Design
Design Firm
Giordano Kearfott Design
Designers
Susan Giordanc, Lee Ater

1007 Tower Building
1809 Seventh Avenue
Seattle, WA 98101

206.682.4895
FAX 206.623.8912
WEB belyea.com

belyea

Client
Belyea
Design Firm
Belyea
Designer
Ron Lars Hansen

envisioncreative

design + marketing
1440 terrace drive
tulsa, oklahoma 74104
phone: 918 744-1101
fax: 918 747-0575
envision@webzone.net

the artists formerly known as davies + associates

Client
  Envision Creative
Design Firm **Envision Creative**
Designer
  Bryan Cooper

BEEF... IT'S WHAT'S FOR DINNER.

630 Grand Canyon Drive • Madison, WI 53719 • Phone: 608-833-7177 • Fax: 608-833-4725

Client
  Wisconsin Beef Council
Design Firm
  Kennedy Communications
Designers
  Robin Sweet, Jonathan Reduker

Client
Barbara J. Schulman
Design Firm
John K. Landis Graphic Design
Designer
John K. Landis

Client
Dr. Susan Love
Design Firm
Hershey Associates
Designers
R. Christine Hershey, Lisa Joss

One-eighty Communications letterhead

118 N. STEVENS STREET
SPOKANE WA 99201
509•444•1000
FAX 509•444•1004
WWW.ONEEIGHTY.COM

oneeighty
COMMUNICATIONS

Client
One-eighty Communications
Design Firm
Klundt Hosmer Design
Designers
Darin Klundt, Shirlee Bonifield

PACKET ENGINES
Gigabit Performance. Enterprise Reliability.™

P.O. Box 14497 • Spokane, WA 99214-0497

CORP: (509) 777-7000
FAX: (509) 777-7001
www.packetengines.com

Client
Packet Engines
Design Firm
Klundt Hosmer Design
Designers
Darin Klundt, Shirlee Bonifield

SPECTRUM
PHOTOGRAPHIC & IMAGING

2351 Powell Street Suite 505
San Francisco California 94133
Tel 415.982.2751 Fax 415.982.3514

Client   Spectrum Photographic
Design Firm   **Focus Design**
Designer   Brian Jacobson

BOSTON
Voice & Data

Client   Boston Voice and Data
Design Firm   **ilana design**
Designer   ilana

42 WHITE STREET · BELMONT MA 02478 · FAX 617 489 8717

PHONE 617 489 4690

Good Samaritan Hospice
of Pittsburgh

3500 Brooktree Road, Suite 200 · Wexford, PA 15090
724-933-8888 · 1-800-720-2557 · fax 724-933-8844

Client
  Good Samaritan Hospice
Design Firm
  A to Z communications, inc.
Designer
  Aimee Lazer

Client
  D & D Investments
Design Firm
  Miller & White Adv.
Designers
  Bill White, Jason Hertenstein

LIGHTHOUSE
LANDINGS

8060 MADISON AVENUE
INDIANAPOLIS, IN 46227
PHONE: 317-885-0700
FAX 317-885-1700

Client
Holocaust Resource Center
Design Firm
College Relations Office
Designer
Christine Justice

Client
Maeme Young
Design Firm
Mitten Design
Designers
Marianne Mitten, Audrey Dufresne

Client
Iger/Reed Productions
Design Firm **Pink Coyote Design, Inc.**
Designer
Joel Ponzan

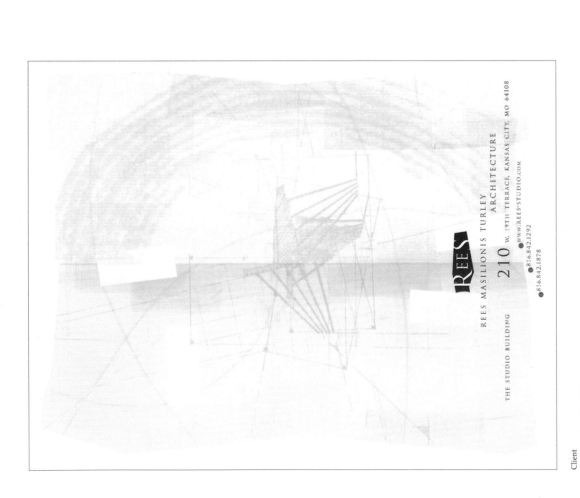

Client
Rees Architecture
Design Firm **Muller + Co.**
Designers
John Muller, Jeff Miller

C I V I A R O S E N B E R G

Studio
535 Albany Street
Boston, Massachusetts 02118

Telephone
617. 262-0348

Home
One Marlborough Street. Apt. 5
Boston, Massachusetts 02116

Client
Civia Rosenberg
Design Firm **ilana design**
Designer
ilana

Client
Simplify
Design Firm
Wechsler Ross & Partners
Designer
Cherese Rambaldi
Art Director
Karen Knorr

Simplify LLC 71 Fifth Avenue, 4th Floor New York, New York 10003-3004
T 212.620.7274 F 212.620.7276 E info@simplify123.com

simplify

135

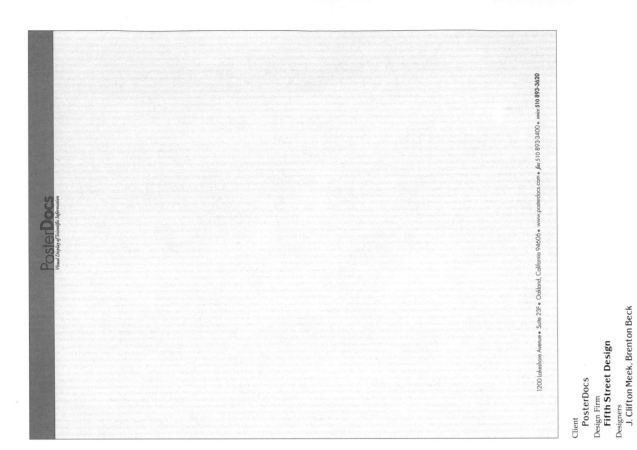

PosterDocs
Visual Display of Scientific Information

1200 Lakeshore Avenue • Suite 23F • Oakland, California 94606 • www.posterdocs.com • *fax* 510 893-3400 • *voice* **510 893-3620**

Client
　PosterDocs
Design Firm
　Fifth Street Design
Designers
　J. Clifton Meek, Brenton Beck

RANDI WOLF • GRAPHIC DESIGNER

RANDI WOLF
DESIGN

ENVIRONMENT

18 CYPRESS COURT • GLASSBORO, NJ 08028
PHONE 609-582-8181 • FAX 609-582-8187

Client
　Randi Wolf Design
Design Firm
　Randi Wolf Design
Designer
　Randi Wolf

Client
Susan A len

P.O. Box 214576 Dallas, TX 75221 214-769-5266 t 214-327-3271 f Art Consultation and Representation

Client
Greenfield Benefits Corporation
Design Firm
Matthew Huberty Design
Designer
Matthew Huberty

6395 Oxbow Bend • Chanhassen, MN 55317 • T 612-401-0290 • F 612-401-0259 • GfieldBen@aol.com

137

Client
Denise Ford
Design Firm **Swieter Design U.S.**
Designer
Mark Ford

DENISE FORD *Agent*
5114 Milam Dallas, Texas 75206
tel 214 821 6788 *fax* 821 0566

Client
Valmontis Bed & Breakfast
Design Firm **Trudy Cole-Zielanski**
Designer
Trudy Cole-Zielanski

Charlottesville, VA
Phone 804-964-1575
Fax 804-964-1385
valmontis@comcin.net

Client
 Church of the Holy Family
Design Firm
 Crowley Webb & Associates
Designer
 Dion Pender

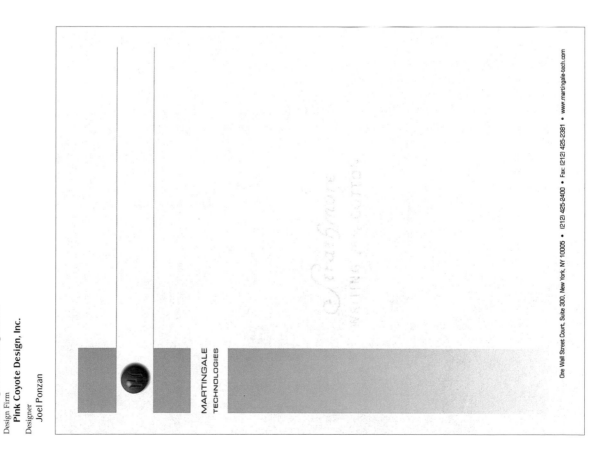

Client
 Martingale Technologies, Inc.
Design Firm
 Pink Coyote Design, Inc.
Designer
 Joel Ponzan

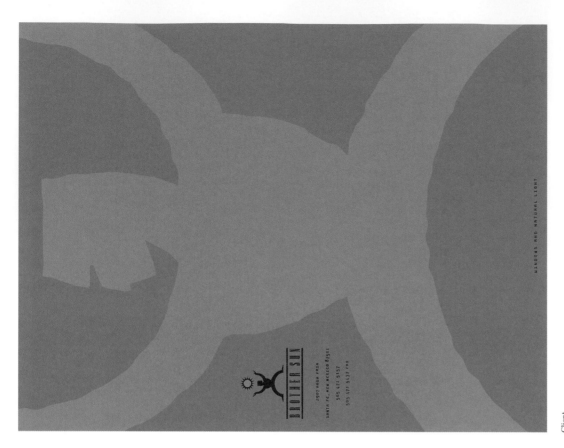

Client
  Brother Sun
Design Firm
  Cisneros Design
Designer
  Brian Hurshman

Client
  Brad Terres Design
Design Firm
  Brad Terres Design
Designer
  Brad Terres

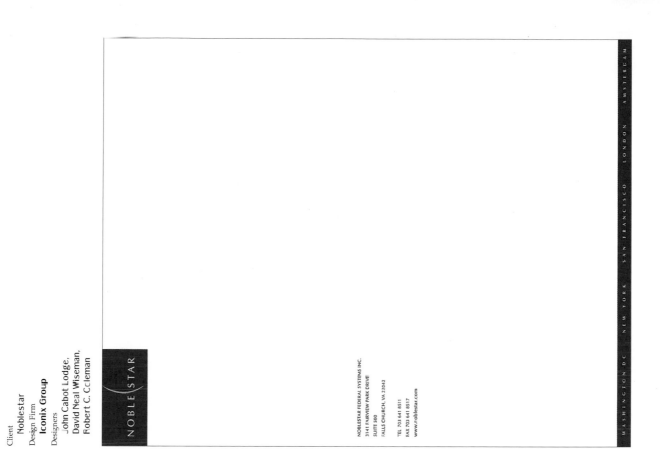

Client
    Noblestar
Design Firm
    Iconix Group
Designers
    John Cabot Lodge,
    David Neal Wiseman,
    Robert C. Coleman

Client
    Mark Sanford Group
Design Firm
    David Day & Associates
Designer
    David Day

Client
YSL Architecture
Design Firm
VR Design
Designer
Victor Rodriguez

Client
PCR
Design Firm
D16 Design
Designer
Amy Decker

142

Clymer Capital
Registered Investment Advisors

CLASSIC CREST

Client
Clymer Capital
Design Firm
Tilka Design
Designer
Mark Mularz

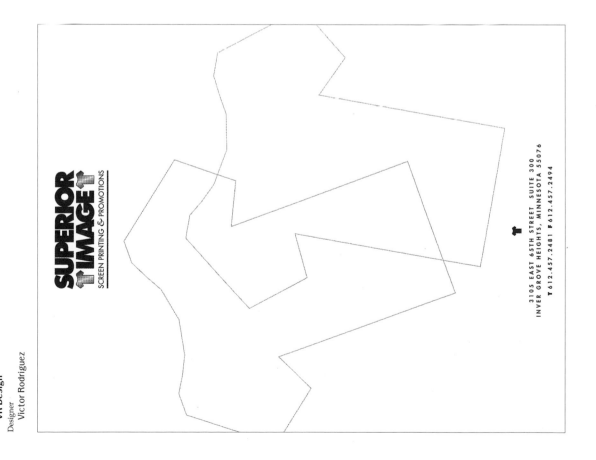

SCREEN PRINTING & PROMOTIONS

3105 EAST 65TH STREET SUITE 300
INVER GROVE HEIGHTS, MINNESOTA 55076
T 612.457.2481 **F** 612.457.2494

Client
Superior Image
Design Firm
VR Design
Designer
Victor Rodriguez

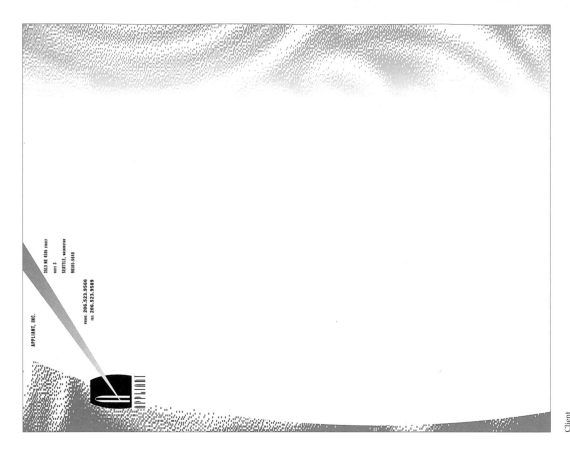

APPLIANT, INC.

3513 NE 45th STREET
SUITE 3
SEATTLE, WASHINGTON
98105-5640

PHONE: 206.523.9566
FAX: 206.523.9589

Client
Appliant, Inc.
Design Firm
David Lemley Design
Designers
David Lemley, Matt Peloza

k
e

A

r

B

BAKER DESIGN ASSOCIATES

Client
Baker Design
Design Firm
Baker Design Associates
Designer
Tom Devine
Creative Director
Gary Baker

ESTANCIA

2776 Barton Creek Blvd.

Austin, Texas 78735

Phone: (512) 306-1785

Fax: (512) 306-8428

Client
Phoenix Property Company
Design Firm
VWA Group
Designer
James Wilson

PACKAGE

CONSULTANTS, PACKAGING DEVELOPMENT AND PRODUCTION
PACK AGE LIMITED THE CABLE BUILDING 611 BROADWAY SUITE 715 NEW YORK CITY 0012
TELEPHONE 212 614 8887 FACSIMILE 212 614 8015 EMAIL RSHAMMAA@PACK-AGE.COM

Client
PackAge
Design Firm
Jeffrey Leder Inc.
Designer
Debra Magnani

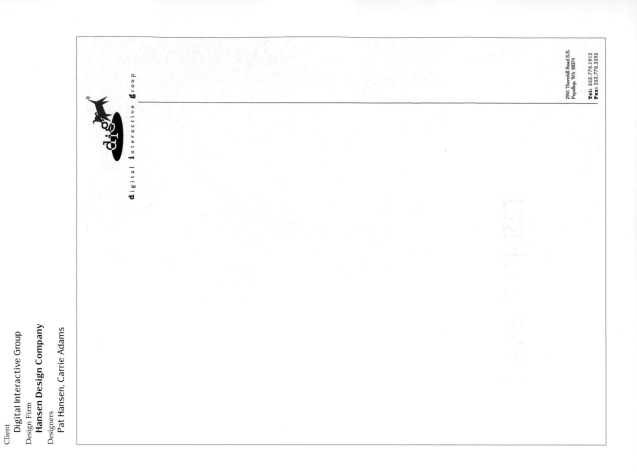

digital interactive group

2901 Thornhill Road S.E.
Puyallup, WA 98374
Tel: 253.770.1912
Fax: 253.770.2695

Client
   Digital Interactive Group
Design Firm
   Hansen Design Company
Designers
   Pat Hansen, Carrie Adams

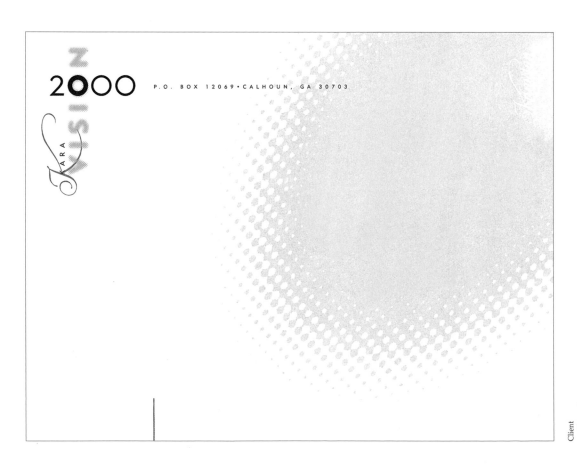

KARA VISION
2OOO
P.O. BOX 12069 • CALHOUN, GA 30703

Client
   Karastan
Design Firm
   MANI Graphics
Designer
   Michael Oberweiser

146

Client
Leap Frog
Design Firm
Cisneros Design
Designer
Harry Forehand III

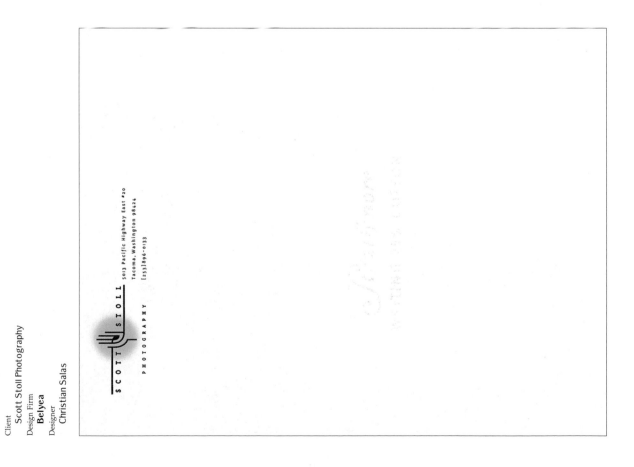

Client
Scott Stoll Photography
Design Firm
Belyea
Designer
Christian Salas

Collins and Associates

Post Office Box 192955
San Francisco, California 9411

tel. 415 695 0830
fax. 415 826 7392

Client
Collins and Associates
Design Firm
Oh Boy, A Design Company
Designer
David Salanitro

Client
Kansas City Blues & Jazz Festival
Design Firm
Muller + Co.
Designers
John Muller, Mark Voss

4200 PENNSYLVANIA AVE. SUITE 230   KANSAS CITY, MO 64111   816.753.3378   FAX: 816.531.2583   www.kcbluesjazz.org

Alice Prussin
Lighting Design

1412 Cypress Street | Berkeley, CA 94703
phone: 510.525.3670
facsimile: 510.525.3472

Client
Alice Prussin Lighting Design
Design Firm
Mitten Design
Designer
Marianne Mitten

MARTY ITTNER

202.328.9039 fax **328.1297** VonBitty@AOL.COM
2227 20th St NW ste 207 Washington DC 20009

Art Direction Graphic Design Marketing

Client
Marty Ittner
Designer
Marty Ittner

149

Client JCLL
Design Firm **Roland Gebhardt Design**
Designers Roland Gebhardt
Concept Carolyn Ehrlich

Jewish Children's Learning Lab
c/o The Board of Jewish Education
426 West 58th Street
New York, NY 10019

Tel: 212 245 8200 Ext. 331
Fax: 212 586 9579
E-mail: jcllcm@aol.com

4250 Glencoe Ave.

Marina del Rey

California 90292

310-306-7979 t

310-306-0992 f

Lincoln Property Company

Client Lincoln Property Company
Design Firm **VWA Group**
Designer Ashley Barron

Client
   C. Taylor Crothers
Design Firm
   Red Herring Design
Designer
   Kristina Dimatteo

Client
   John Buck Company
Design Firm
   Weingart Associates
Designer
   Jamie Anderson

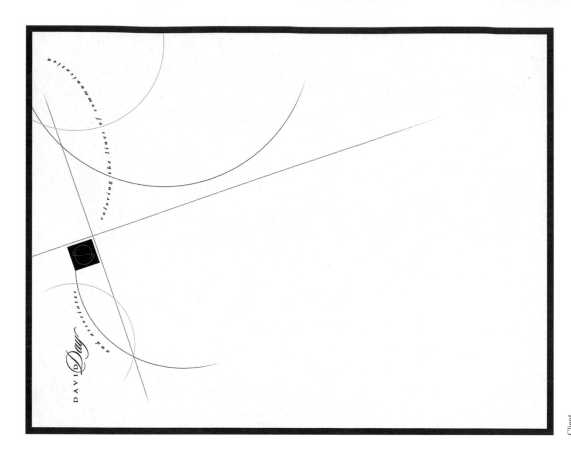

Client
David Day & Associates
Design Firm **David Day & Associates**
Designer
David Day

Client
Art Plus Technology
Design Firm **Art Plus Technology**
Designers
Gary Clark, Robert Linsky

apt art plus technology for business™

♦ 123 N. Washington St., Suite 401, Boston, MA 02114-2113
♦ tel: 617-646-4000 fax: 617-646-4040
♦ web: www.aptboston.com

Improving customer and corporate communications through the effective application of design, technology, and education

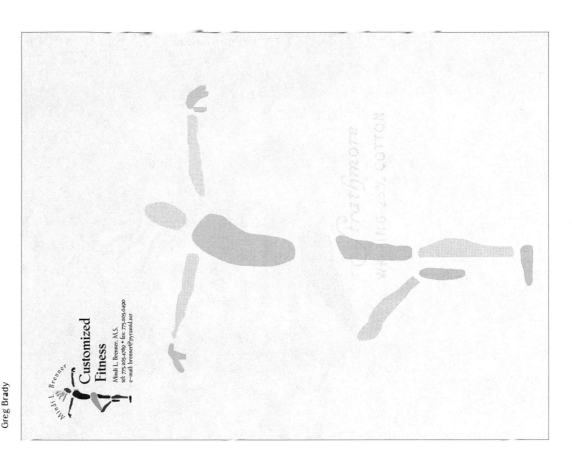

Client
Mindi L. Brenner
Design Firm
Stockdale & Crum
Designer
Greg Brady

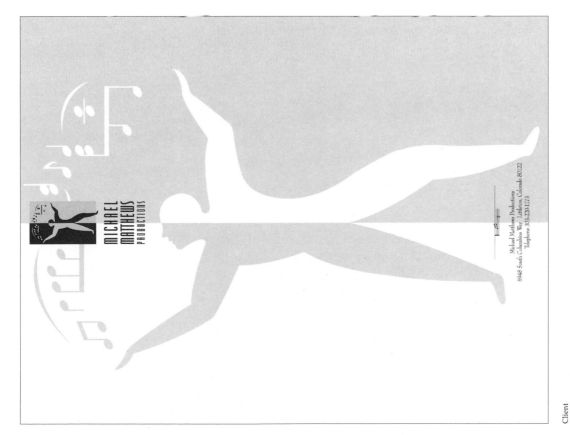

Client
Michael Matthews Productions
Design Firm
David Day & Associates
Designer
Joyce Augustinis

Client
Spoke
Design Firm
Trace
Designer
Aldis Strazdins

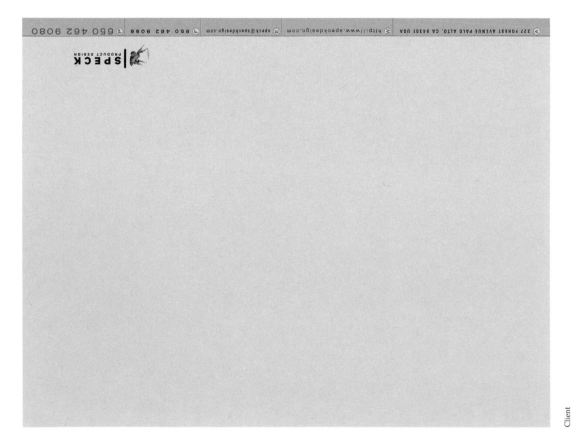

Client
Speck Product Design
Design Firm
Tolleson Design
Designers
Steve Tolleson, Mark Winn

154

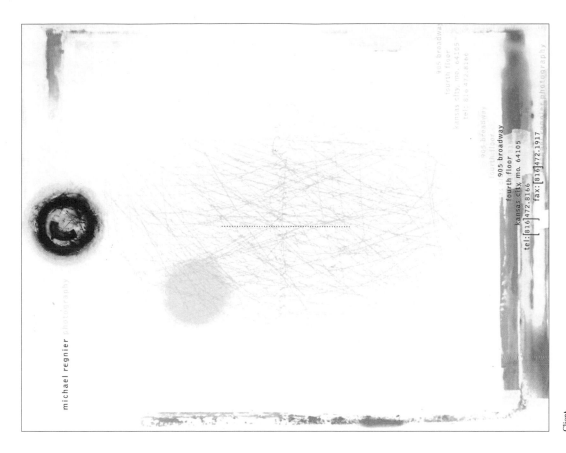

michael regnier photography

905 broadway
fourth floor
kansas city, mo. 64105
tel: [816] 472.8166
fax: [816] 472.1917

Client
   Michael Regnier Photography
Design Firm
   Muller + Co.
Designer
   John Muller, Jeⁿ Miller

cre•a•tive (adj.)
Productive, artistic, inventive: A visual thinker capable of handling the responsibilities
of multiple projects simultaneously from start to finish. See also **Kimberlee Davis,**
189 Littleton Road, Apt. #89, Parsippany, NJ 07054, (973) 335-4914

Client
   Kim Davis
Designer
   Kim Davis

Client
Chase Communications
Design Firm **DesignTribe**
Designer
Mark Marinozzi, Dennis Pettigrew

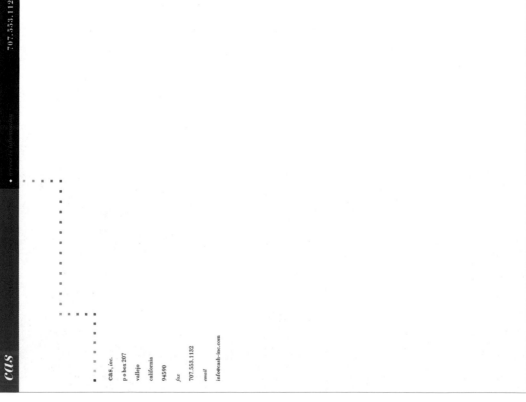

Client
CAS
Design Firm **Fifth Street Design**
Designer
J. Clifton Meek, Brenton Beck

Client
Agility
Design Firm
Design Kitchen
Designer
Kira Bevic

Client
Linda Dickerson Interiors
Design Firm
**Peter Taflan Marketing
Communications, Inc.**
Designer
Janssen Strother

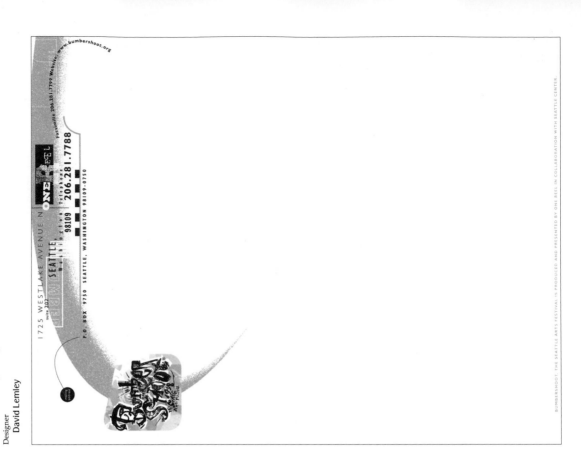

Client
One Reel
Design Firm
David Lemley Design
Designer
David Lemley

Client
MLSPA
Design Firm
Grafik Communications
Designers
Jonathan Amen, David Collins, Judy Kirpich

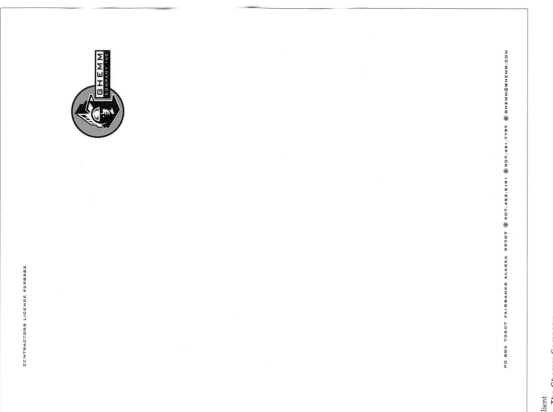

PO BOX 70507 FAIRBANKS ALASKA 99707 ✆ 907.452.5191 ✆ 907.451.7797 ✉ GHEMM@GHEMM.COM

Client   The Ghemm Company
Design Firm   **Visual Asylum**
Designers   Amy Jo Levine, MaeLin Levine, Joel Sotelo

Client   Big Daddy Photography
Design Firm   **Sayles Graphic Design**
Designer   John Sayles

5703 NW Second Avenue Suite 2
Des Moines, Iowa 50313

phone (515) 243-0718
fax (515) 243-0136

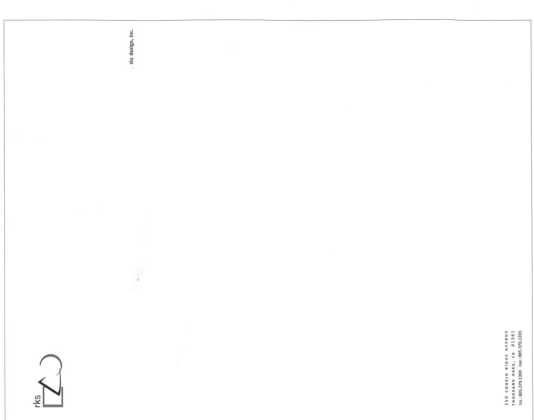

350 CONEJO RIDGE AVENUE
THOUSAND OAKS, CA 91361
TEL: 805.370.1200 FAX: 805.370.1203

Client
RKS Design, Inc.
Design Firm
RKS Design, Inc.

601 EAST LOCKWOOD { ST.LOUIS, MISSOURI } 63119

{ [FAX] 314·962·7718
wWw·alpineshOp·Com [web]

314·862·7715
(phOnE)

Client
Alpine Shop
Design Firm
Phoenix Creative, St. Louis
Designer
Deborah Finkelstein

Client
New World Post Productions
Design Firm
Phoenix Creative, St. Louis
Designer
Deborah Finkelstein

Client
Campbell Design
Design Firm
Michael Patrick Partners
Designer
Bernie Wooster

Client
Creative Fusions
Design Firm
Tim Girvin Design, Inc.
Designer
Kim Edberg

Salzburg Family University
July 5 - 11, 1998

University Chairmen
Peter & Analía Whitehead
Nassau, Bahamas

Education Chairmen
John & Faye Fischer
Boulder, Colorado

Off-Sites Chairmen
Hugh & Rebecca Winters
Toronto, Canada

Youth Chairmen
Richard & Carla McCombe
Nassau, Bahamas

Hospitality Chairmen
Bob & Sandy Mungels
Sao Paulo, Brazil

Social Chairmen
Victor & Panayota Antippas
Athens, Greece

Transportation Chairmen
Ulrich & Gabriele Stepski
Hald, Austria

Advisors
Count & Countess
Manfred Clary
und Aldringen
Salzburg, Austria

Baron & Baroness
Maximilian Mayr-Melnhof
Salzburg, Austria

YPO International President
Steven & Michelle Karol
Boston, Massachusetts

Young Presidents' Organization
Hickok Center
451 S. Decker Drive
Irving, Texas 75062 U.S.A.
1.972.680.4600
1.972.650.4777 fax
1.800.773.7976

www.ypo.org

Client
Young Presidents' Organization
Design Firm
Swieter Design U.S.
Designers
John Swieter, Cameron Smith

162

HEALTHLINE | MANAGEMENT℠

1509 WASHINGTON AVENUE SUITE 800 ST.LOUIS, MO 63103-1803
tel 314 241 2345 *or* 800 443 3901 *fax* 314 206 4040 *web* WWW.HMISTL.COM

The nation's premier comprehensive management services organization...serving the health care community since 1985

PHYSICIAN—J & APN/PA PLACEMENT • PERMANENT & INTERIM PHYSICIAN STAFFING • EMERGENCY DEPARTMENT STAFFING • PRACTICE ASSESSMENTS
PRACTICE MANAGEMENT • HUMAN RESOURCES MANAGEMENT • BUSINESS PLANNING • STRATEGIC PLANNING • BILLING MANAGEMENT
NETWORK DEVELOPMENT • CREDENTIAL VERIFICATION SERVICES • RESEARCH & MARKETING SERVICES • INFORMATION SYSTEMS CONSULTING

Client
HealthLine Management
Design Firm
Phoenix Creative, St. Louis
Designer
Steve Wienke

Client
Pinpoint Corporation
Design Firm
Design Continuum Inc
Designers
Richard Davia, Michelle Tsay

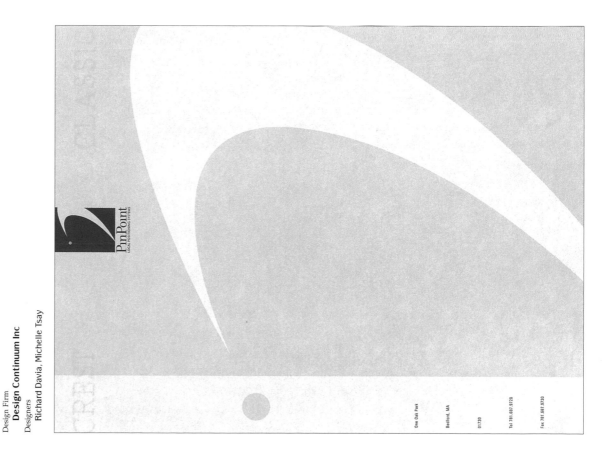

PinPoint
LOCAL POSITIONING SYSTEMS

One Oak Park

Bedford, MA

01730

Tel 781.687.9720

Fax 781.687.9720

Client
Genisys
Design Firm
Marion Graphics, L.C.
Designer
Marion Graphics

Client
St. Louis Rams
Design Firm
Phoenix Creative, St. Louis
Designer
Kathy Wilkinson

Client
1998 Iowa State Fair Blue Ribbon Foundation
Design Firm **Sayles Graphic Design**
Designer
John Sayles

Client
Eden Bioscience
Design Firm **Tim Girvin Design, Inc.**
Designer
Jennifer Bartlett

165

Client
CAG Design
Design Firm **CAG Design**
Designer
Kristin Levitskie

Client
Marché
Design Firm **Funk & Associates**
Designer
Beverly Soasey

4N474 PATHFINDER DRIVE
ELBURN, ILLINOIS 60119

P H O N E
6 3 0 . 3 6 5 . 2 6 4 0
F A X
6 3 0 . 3 6 5 . 9 5 4 0

Client
    Peich
Design Firm
    Z·D Studios, Inc.
Designer
    Mark Schmitz

Client
    Veeder & Perman
Design Firm
    MANI Graphics
Designer
    Dina Sporer

568 BROADWAY #703   NEW YORK, NY 10012   TEL 212.966.3759   FAX 212.966.3295

ZEUM

Client
Yerba Buena Gardens
Design Firm
Cahan & Associates
Designer
Ben Pham

Client
Microsoft
Design Firm
GA Design
Designers
Klindt Parker, Kurt Niedermeier

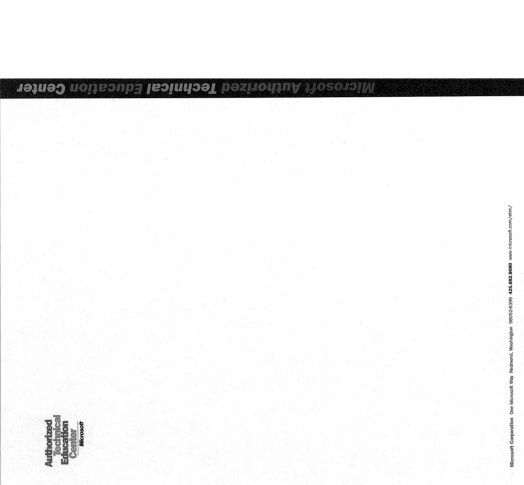

Microsoft Authorized **Technical** Education **Center**

Authorized
Technical
Education
Center
Microsoft

Microsoft Corporation One Microsoft Way Redmond, Washington 98052-6399 **425.882.8080** www.microsoft.com/atec/

Client
Aquium
Design Firm
Aquium
Designer
Keith D. Roueché, Patricia Murphey,
Robin Lowey, John Sigler

Client
Michael Doret Graphic Design
Design Firm
Michael Doret Graphic Design
Designer
Michael Doret

Client
Scottsdale Waterfront
Design Firm
After Hours Creative
Designers
After Hours Creative

Client
Kay Chernush Photography
Design Firm
Iconix Group
Designer
Mary Parsons

170

Client

Splendid Salmon Corp

Head of the Harbor
11-15 Parker Street
Gloucester, MA 01930

Tel: 978.281.7632
Fax: 978.281.7692

office@splendidsalmon.com
www.splendidsalmon.com

Client
Splendid Salmon■
Design Firm
Heyck Design
Designer
Edith Heyck
Art Director
Bruce DeMustchine

Jane Brown Interiors

32 Hillcrest Meadows ~ Rolling Hills Estates, CA 90274 ~ 310.544.0625 ~ Fax 310.544.0635

Client
Jane Brown Interiors
Design Firm
Julia Tam Design
Designer
Julia Tam

DRIVE COMMUNICATIONS   133 WEST 19TH STREET   FIFTH FLOOR   NEW YORK NEW YORK 10011

TELEPHONE 212 989 5103   FACSIMILE 212 929 3391   E-MAIL DRYCOM@AOL.COM

Client
Drive Communications
Design Firm
Drive Communications
Designer
Michael Graziolo

ideas shaping business

PERCEIVE

249 OCEAN BLVD, SUITE 500
LONG BEACH, CA 90802-4813
perceivellc.com

TEL 562.951.1155
FAX 562.901.1849

Design Firm
Perceive
Designer
Jamie Graupner

172

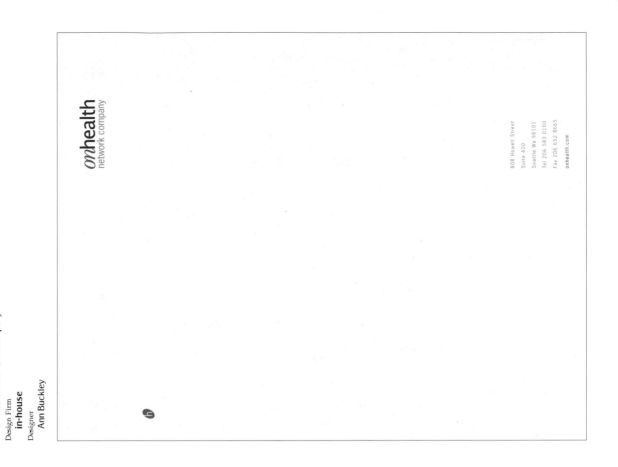

onhealth
network company

808 Howell Street
Suite 400
Seattle Wa 98101
Tel 206 583 0100
Fax 206 652 8665
onhealth.com

Client On Health Network Company
Design Firm **in-house**
Designer Ann Buckley

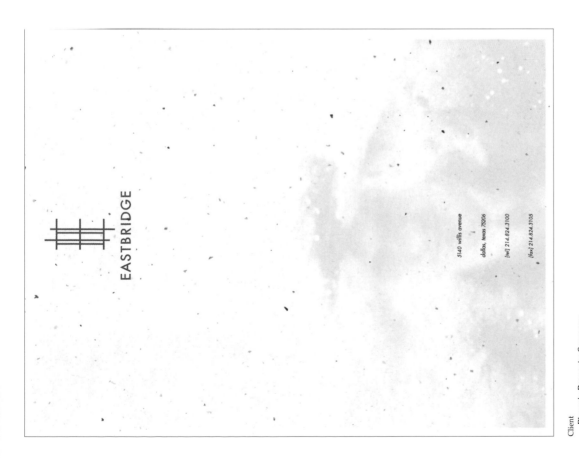

EASTBRIDGE

5140 willis avenue

dallas, texas 75206

[tel] 214.824.3100

[fax] 214.824.3105

Client Phoenix Property Company
Design Firm **VWA Group**
Designer James Wilson

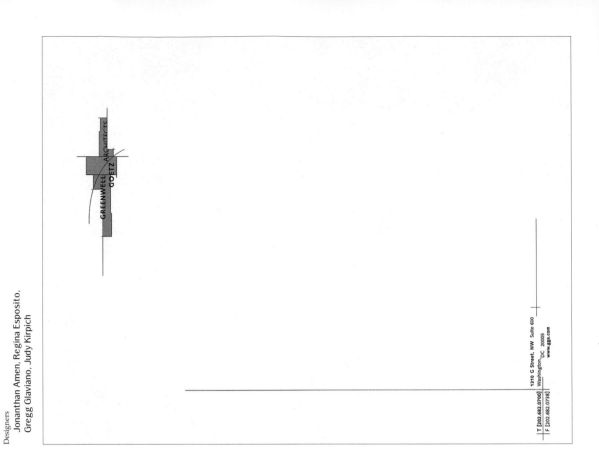

Client
Greenwall Goetz Architects
Design Firm
Grafik Communications
Designers
Jonanthan Amen, Regina Esposito,
Gregg Glaviano, Judy Kirpich

GREENWELL
GOETZ ARCHITECTS

1310 G Street, NW Suite 600
Washington DC 20005
www.ggx.com

T [202.682.0790]
F [202.682.0738]

PHONE 225.635.4107 • **FAX** 225.635.6067 • **EMAIL** gbuttons@bsf.net

POST OFFICE BOX 1689 • 9814 ROYAL STREET • ST. FRANCISVILLE, LOUISIANA 70775

Grandmother's
BUTTONS

GB Collection
REPLICAS FROM
THE GRANDMOTHER'S
BUTTONS COLLECTION

DIVISIONS OF PROSPERITY AT ROYAL, INC.

Client
Grandmother's Buttons
Design Firm
DSI/LA
Designer
Nicole Duet

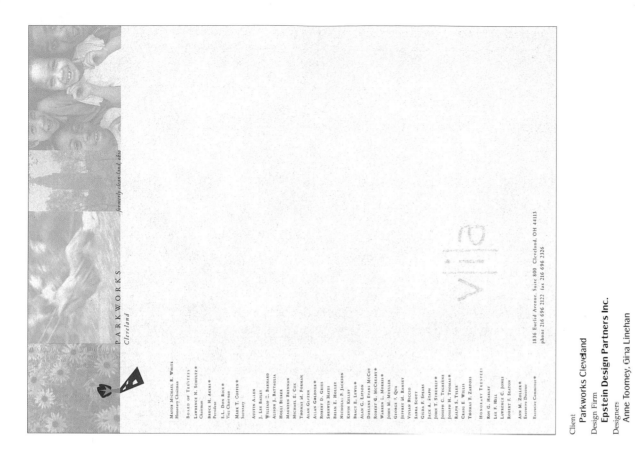

Client
Archipelago Films
Design Firm
Drive Communications
Designer
Michael Graziolo

Client
Parkworks Cleveland
Design Firm
Epstein Design Partners Inc.
Designers
Anne Toomey, Gina Linehan

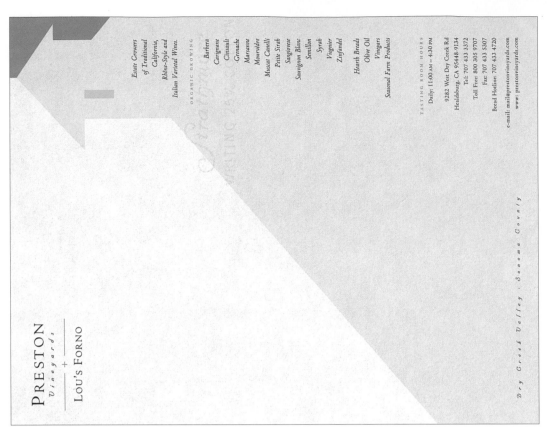

PRESTON
Vineyards
+
LOU'S FORNO

*Estate Growers
of Traditional
California,
Rhône-Style and
Italian Varietal Wines.*

ORGANIC GROWING

Barbera
Carignane
Cinsault
Grenache
Marsanne
Mourvèdre
Muscat Canelli
Petite Sirah
Sangiovese
Sauvignon Blanc
Semillon
Syrah
Viognier
Zinfandel

Hearth Breads
Olive Oil
Vinegars
Seasonal Farm Products

TASTING ROOM HOURS

Daily: 11:00 AM – 4:30 PM

9282 West Dry Creek Rd
Healdsburg, CA 95448-9134
Tel: 707 433 3372
Toll Free: 800 305 9707
Fax: 707 433 5307
Bread Hotline: 707 433 4720
e-mail: mail@prestonvineyards.com
www: prestonvineyards.com

Dry Creek Valley · Sonoma County

Client
Preston Vineyards
Design Firm
Buttitta Design
Designer
Patti Buttitta

Client
Global Pacific Information Services, Inc.
Design Firm
Bloch + Coulter Design Group
Designers
Heather Gondek, Thomas Bloch, Victoria Coulter

Global Pacific Information Services, Inc.

new paradigm for business

27131 Calle Arroyo, Suite 1703   San Juan Capistrano, CA 92675   tel 949.248.2404   fax 949.248.2413   e-mail administrator@virtualceo.com

PRIME COMPANIES, INC.

155 Montgomery Street   San Francisco   TELEPHONE 415 398 4242   www.primecompanies.com
Suite 426   California 94404-4109   FACSIMILE 415 398 4244

Client
Prime Companies, Inc.
Design Firm
Lamfers & Associates
Designers
Missy Nery, Debra Lamfers

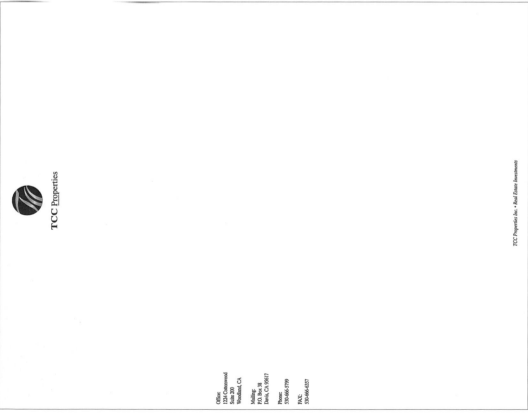

TCC Properties

Office:
1224 Cottonwood
Suite 200
Woodland, CA

Mailing:
P.O. Box 38
Davis, CA 95617

Phone:
530-666-5799

FAX:
530-666-6357

TCC Properties Inc. • Real Estate Investments

Client
TCC Properties
Design Firm
BauMac Communications
Designer
Tara Baumann

NOELKER
AND HULL
ASSOCIATES, INC
ARCHITECTS

Client
    Noelker and Hull Associates
Design Firm
    Dean Design
Designer
    Lori Hess

30 West King Street Chambersburg, PA 17201-1540   TEL 717.263.8464   FAX 717.263.6031   info@noelkerhull.com   www.noelkerhull.com

YOSEMITE

YOSEMITE CONCESSION SERVICES CORPORATION
A DELAWARE NORTH COMPANY
Yosemite National Park, California 95389
209 372-1014 tel
209 372-1064 fax
www.yosemitepark.com

Client
    Yosemite Concession Services
Design Firm
    Boling Associates
Designer
    Jeff Barkema

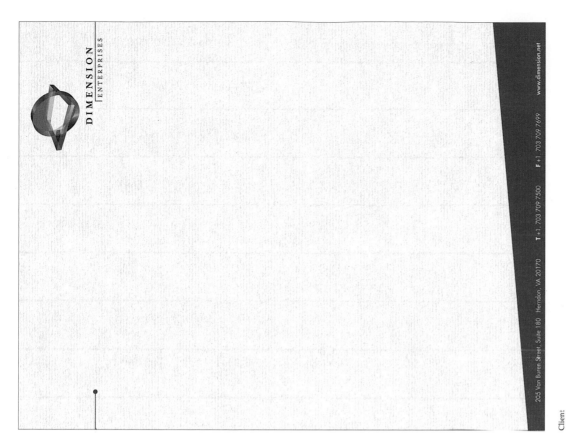

Client
Kaelson Company
Design Firm
latitude
Designers
Pete Sockwell, Paul vonHeeder

Client:
Dimension Enterprises
Design Firm
Gr8
Designer
Rob **Rhinehart**

DIMENSION | ENTERPRISES

205 Van Buren Street, Suite 180   Herndon, VA 20170   **T** +1. 703 709 7500   **F** +1. 703 709 7699   www.dimension.net

KAELSON COMPANY
INTEGRATED LANDSCAPES

3015 CANTON STREET . DALLAS, TEXAS 75226 . PHONE 214.741.1111 . FAX 214.741.9999

179

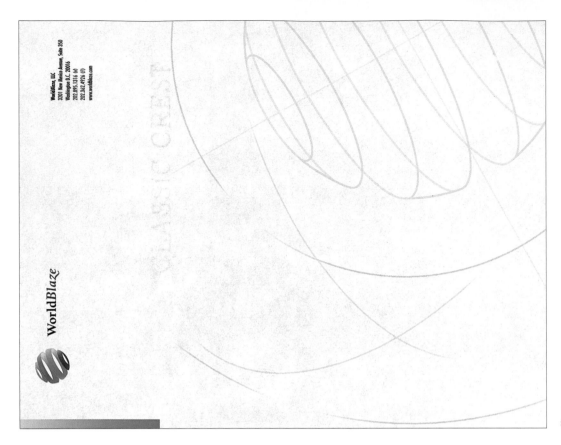

WorldBlaze

WorldBlaze, LLC
3201 New Mexico Avenue, Suite 350
Washington D.C. 20016
202.895.1316 (v)
202.362.4926 (f)
www.worldblaze.com

Client
WorldBlaze
Design Firm
California Design Int'l
Designers
Linda Kelley, Dan Liew

A LONZO
ENVIRONMENTAL PRINTING

3266 Investment Blvd.
Hayward · California
94545-3807
TEL 510.293.0522
FAX 510.293.3958
PRINTED ON RECYCLED PAPER
USING SOY BASE LINKS

Client
Alonzo Printing
Design Firm
Shelby Designs & Illustrates
Designers
Shelby Putnam Tupper, Jill Sanford

Client
Photo Communications
Design Firm
Gr8
Designers
Alicia Leaf, Morton Jackson,
Lisa Wurfl-Roeca

Client
Infinet Incorporated
Design Firm
Cathey Associates, Inc.
Designers
Gordon Cathey, Isabel Gracia

Client
Reno Tahoe Territory
Design Firm
Stockdale & Crum
Designer
Suzanne J. Stockdale

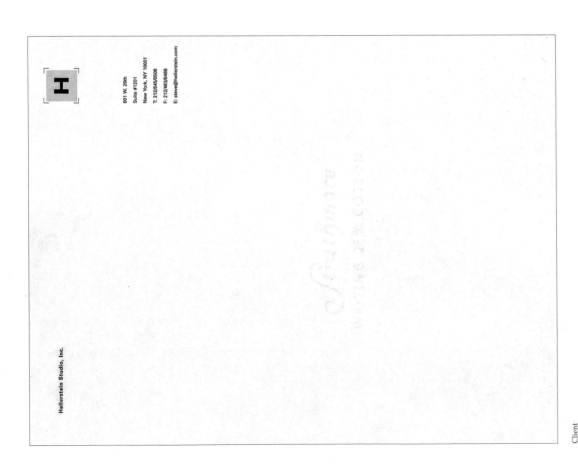

Client
Hellerstein Studio
Design Firm
Taylor Design
Designer
Nora Vaivads

Icon Graphics Inc.

ICON

phone (716) 325-1530

fax (716) 325-1532

277 Alexander Street   Suite 400   Rochester, New York 14607

Client
Icon Graphics Inc.
Design Firm
Icon Graphics Inc.

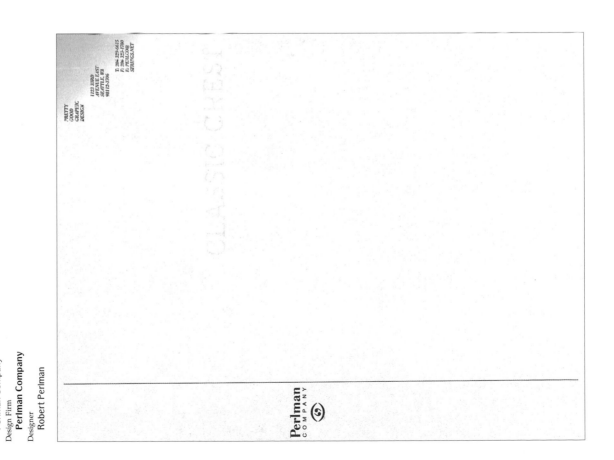

PRETTY
GOOD
GRAPHIC
DESIGN

1123 33RD
AVENUE EAST
SEATTLE, WA
98112-3706

T: 206-229-6615
F: 206-325-1780
E: PGD@.DOB
STRIP2G.NET

CLASSIC CREST

Perlman
COMPANY

Client
Perlman Company
Design Firm
Perlman Company
Designer
Robert Perlman

13906 GOLD CIRCLE

SUITE 201

OMAHA, NE 68144

TEL 402.330.2520

FAX 402.330.2445

1.888.656.0634

WWW.SAMSONMUSIC.COM

Client
Gold Circle Entertainment
Design Firm **Webster Design Associates**
Designers
Sean Heisler, Dave Webster

clear blue sky PRODUCTIONS
Post Office Box 52930
Bellevue, WA 98015-2930
425.990.0577/phone 425.990.0578fax
www.clearblueskyfilms.com

Client
Clear Blue Sky Productions
Design Firm **Werkhaus Design**
Designer
Christina Stein

184

Client
  MachineHead, Inc.
Design Firm
  EAT Advertising & Design, Inc.
Designers
  Patrice Eilts-Jobe, Paul Prato

715 E. 18TH STREET
KANSAS CITY, MO 64108

PH 816.474.7774
FX 816.531.7593

drvolvo@primary.net

MSI Resources, Inc.
1024 North Boulevard
P.O. Box 4029
Oak Park, IL 60303

708.524.9622 main
708.524.9630 fax
www.msiresources.com

Client
  MSI Resources, Inc.
Design Firm
  Connelly Design
Designers
  Liz Goodwin, Susan Graim

Client
　Kenmark
Design Firm
　Gensler Studio 585
Designers
　Chris Seager, Jane Brady, Cathy Noe

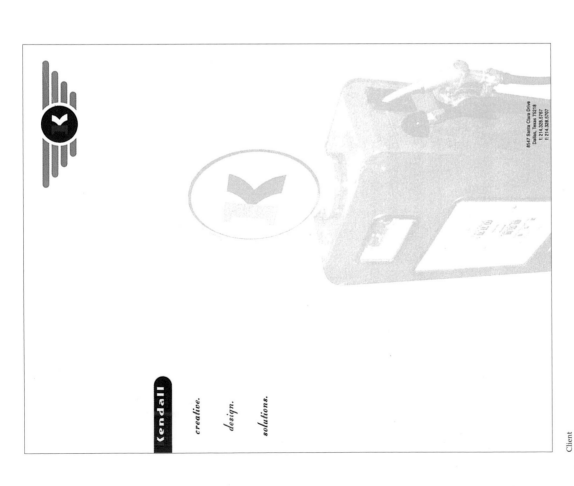

Client
　Kendall Creative Shop
Design Firm
　Kendall Creative Shop
Designer
　Mark K. Platt

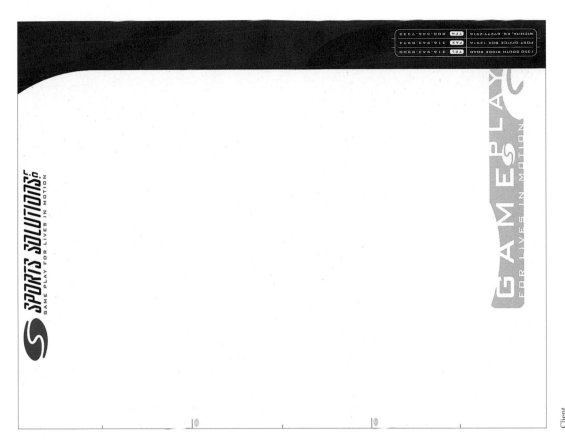

Client
Sports Solutions
Design Firm **Insight Design Communications**
Designer
Chris Parks

Client
Wells Fargo innoVisions
Design Firm **Hornall Anderson Design Works**
Designers
Jack Anderson, Kathy Saito, Alan Copeland

innoVisions, LLC

111 SUTTER ST

17TH FLOOR

SAN FRANCISCO CA

9 4 1 0 4

inno-vision.com

A Wells Fargo / Mr. Payroll Partnership

187

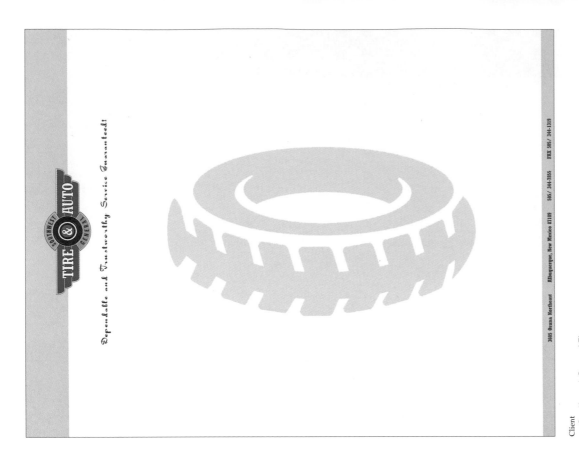

Dependable and Trustworthy Service Guaranteed!

3605 Osuna Northeast   Albuquerque, New Mexico 87109   505/ 344-7855   FAX 505/ 344-1319

Client
   Southwest General Tire
Design Firm
   A-Hill Design
Designer
   Sandy Hill, Emma Roberts

1501 Monroe Street
Madison WI 53711-2020
phone:608.256.35MM
fax:608.259.0559

Client
   Pop Pictures
Design Firm
   Z·D Studios, Inc.
Designer
   Mark Schmitz

Client
Design Goes Inc.
Design Firm
Design Goes Inc.
Designers
Robert Goes, Norman Garbaccio

2073 Outpost Drive • Hollywood • California 90068
Telephone: 213.876.9398 • Fax: 213.436.2705 • Online: designgoes@aol.com

M A H L U M

architects

JOHN MAHLUM • VINCENT NORDFORS • PATRICK GORDON • MICHAEL SMITH • MICHAEL YATES

2505
Third ave.
SUITE 219
Seattle, WA
98121
206.441.4151
206.441.0478
f

Client
Mahlum
Design Firm
Hornall Anderson Design Works
Designers
Jack Anderson,
Heidi Favour, Margaret Long

Client
Tim Whalen
Design Firm
Bullet Communications, Inc.
Designer
Tim Scott

Client
Humanities Iowa
Design Firm
Strong Productions
Designers
Brian Cox, Matt Doty

Client
Webster Design Associates
Design Firm
Webster Design Associates
Designers
Dave Webster, Sean Heisler

5060 Dodge Street   Omaha, NE 68132

TEL 402.551.0503   FAX 402.551.1410

www.websterdesign.com

Client
The Benefits Group
Design Firm
Connolly & Connolly, Inc.
Designer
Elaine Rentz

TheBenefitsGroup

Life
Disability
Group
Pensions

677 South Main Street
Post Office Box 2112
Cheshire, CT 06410
t: 203-250-7880
f: 203-271-0868
e: benefits_group@snet.net

Securities through...Filion Financial Services, Inc.
Member NASD/SIPC, 215 Church Street
New Haven, CT 06510; t: (203) 865-0666

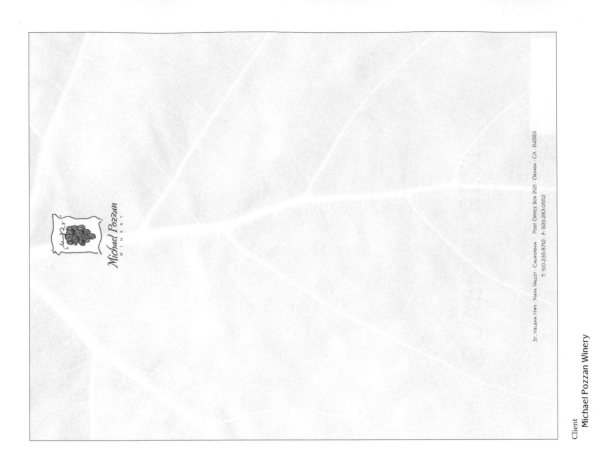

Client
  Michael Pozzan Winery
Design Firm
  Shelby Designs & Illustrates
Designers
  Shelby Putnam Tupper, Susan Rothman

St. Helena Hwy · Napa Valley · California   Post Office Box 2121 · Orinda · CA · 94563
T: 510 235-8712 · F: 925 283-0552

Client
  The Office Works
Design Firm
  Design Room
Designers
  Jennifer Hargreaves, Chad Gordon

The Office Works
Administrative Services for Business

P.O. Box

38218

Olmsted Falls

Ohio

44138

Phone

440~235~6886

Fax

440~235~6860

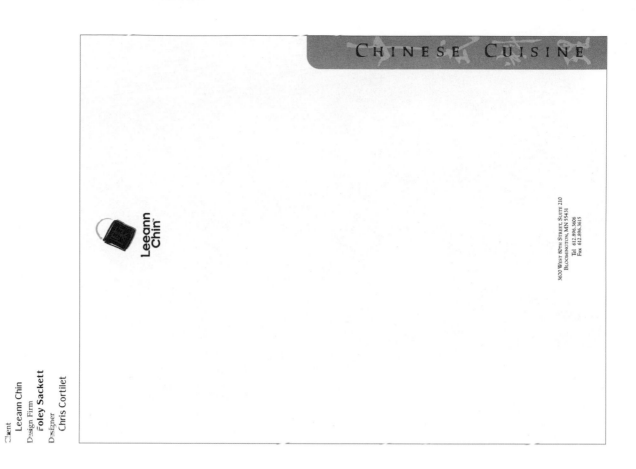

Leeann Chin

3600 WEST 80TH STREET, SUITE 210
BLOOMINGTON, MN 55431
Tel 612.896.3606
Fax 612.896.3615

Client
  Leeann Chin
Design Firm
  Foley Sackett
Designer
  Chris Cortilet

STORE

7700 WISCONSIN AVENUE • BETHESDA • MARYLAND • 20814

Client
  Discovery Communications Inc.
Design Firm
  Discovery Design Group
Designer
  Mike Zizza
Art Director
  Janet Daniel

Client
Custom Business Interiors
Design Firm
Creative Dynamics Inc.
Designer
Eddie Roberts

Client
A-Hill Design
Design Firm
A-Hill Design
Designers
Sandy Hill, Emma Roberts

BEAUTIQUE
DAY SPA & SALON

In The Village • 2507 Times Blvd. • Houston, Texas 77005 • p 713.526.1126 • f 713.523.7014

Client
Beautique Day Spa & Salon
Design Firm
VR Design
Designer
Suzy Ginsburg

tech2me

7549 Richmond Hill NW
Albuquerque New Mexico
87120-4557
505/ 490-4022
fax/ 490-4024

Client
Tech 2 Me
Design Firm
A-Hill Design
Designers
Sandy Hill, Emma Roberts

Nomenon
Naming and Identity Services

25½ Grant Street • Cambridge, MA 02138
Phone 617.864.3113 • Fax 617.864.3116
www.nomenon.com • Free 888.811.NAME

Client
   Nomenon
Design Firm
   Anastasia Design
Designer
   Anastasia Tanis

Client
   TPC
Design Firm
   Phillips Design Group
Designer
   Susan Logcher

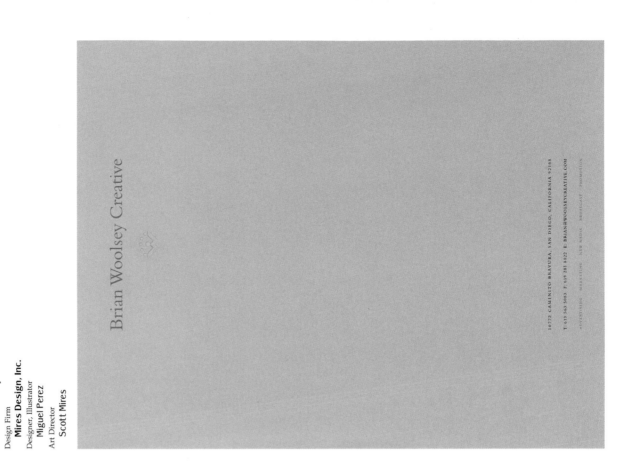

Client
Brian Woolsey
Design Firm
Mires Design, Inc.
Designer, Illustrator
Miguel Perez
Art Director
Scott Mires

Design Firm
Z·D Studios, Inc.
Designer
Mark W. Schmitz

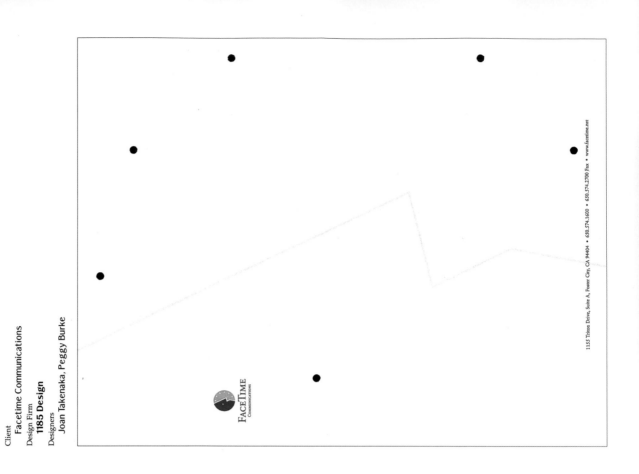

Client
Facetime Communications
Design Firm
1185 Design
Designers
Joan Takenaka, Peggy Burke

1155 Triton Drive, Suite A, Foster City, CA 94404 • 650.574.1600 • 650.574.2700 Fax • www.facetime.net

Client
Michael Luis & Associates
Design Firm
Art O Mat Design
Designers
Mark Kaufman, Jacki McCarthy

P.O. Box 15 ▪ Medina, WA 98039 ▪ (425) 453-5123 ▪ Fax (425) 462-0776 ▪ mluis@oeaner.com

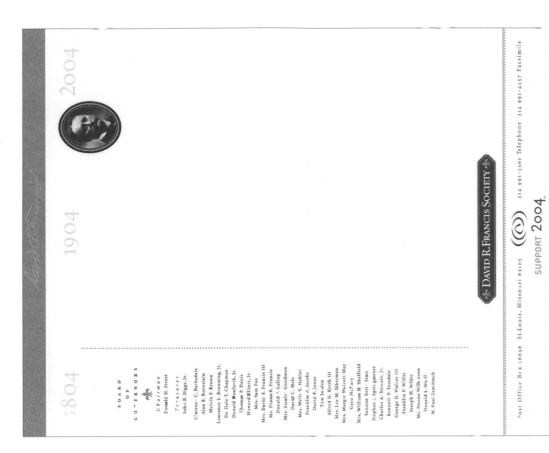

Client
David R. Francs Society
Design Firm
Phoenix Creative, St. Louis
Designer
Ed Mantels-Seeker

Client
Northstar Management Co.
Design Firm
CUBE Advertising & Design
Designers
David Chiow, Matt Marino

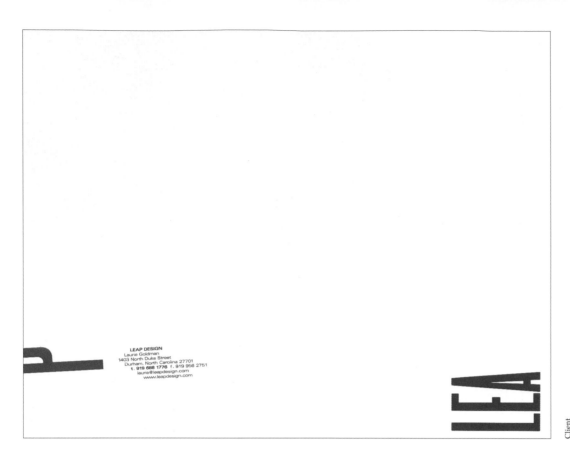

LEAP DESIGN
Laurie Goldman
1403 North Duke Street
Durham, North Carolina 27701
t. **919 688 1776** f. 919 956 2751
laurie@leapdesign.com
www.leapdesign.com

Client
  Leap Design
Design Firm
  Leap Design
Designer
  Laurie Goldman

Client
  Cisneros Design
Design Firm
  Cisneros Design
Designers
  Fred, Brian, Harry 3, Eric,
  Heather, Allane, Fred Sr.

D

A

B

Client
  Kimpton Hotel Group
Design Firm **Hunt Weber Clark Associates**
Designers
  Nancy Hunt-Weber,
  Daniel Ross, Christine Chung

Beckson Design Associates 933 North La Brea Ave. Suite 300 Los Angeles, CA 90038 323.874.6144 Fax 323.874.6148 info@becksondesign.com

Client
  Beckson Design Associates
Design Firm
  James Robie Design Associates
Designer
  Wayne Fujita

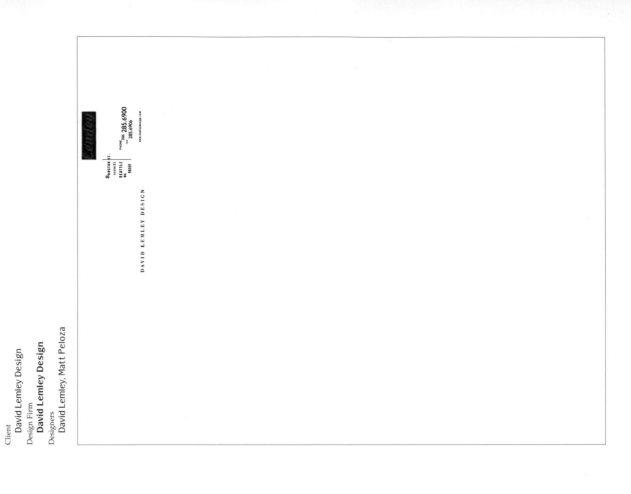

Client
David Lemley Design
Design Firm **David Lemley Design**
Designers
David Lemley, Matt Peloza

Client
Safeguard Health Enterprises, Inc.
Design Firm **Baker Design Associates**
Designer
Louis D'Esposito
Creative Director
Gary Baker

comunica

Comunica/Learning Partners, Inc.
1204 San José Avenue
Santa Fe, New Mexico 87505
505.820.7651
fax 505.982.7353
email comunica@trail.com

Client
Comunica Learning Partners
Design Firm
Cisneros Design
Designer
Fred Cisneros

INSTRUMENTATION METRICS

Protocol Writing
25% Cotton

2085 TECHNOLOGY CIRCLE
SUITE 102
TEMPE, ARIZONA 85284
TEL: 602 755 9483
FAX: 602 755 9832

Client
Instrumentation Metrics, Inc.
Design Firm
Design Continuum Inc
Designers
Tina Hong, Christen Kucharik

MIDWEST
CAPITAL

7316 Grover Drive
Omaha, Nebraska 68124-3330
402.571.1505
Fax: 402.571.0073

Securities Offered Through
GWR Investments, Inc.
MEMBER NASD / SIPC

Client
Midwest Capital
Design Firm
David Day & Associates
Designer
David Day

HSB

Hengst Streff Bajko Architects

1250 Old River Road
Suite 207
Cleveland Ohio 44113-1243
e-mail: hsb@cyberdrive.net
216 566 0440 f
216 566 0229 t

Client
Hengst Streff Bajko Architects
Design Firm
Nesnadny + Schwartz
Designers
Timothy Lachina, Michelle Moehler

UJA-FEDERATION OF NEW YORK

Client
United Jewish Association-Federation
Design Firm
Tim Girvin Design, Inc.
Designer
Brian Boram

A Tradition of Caring

Brand Book

brochures

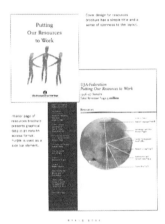

Client
Staples, Inc.
Design Firm
BrandEquity International
Designers
Anne McCuen, Steve Smith

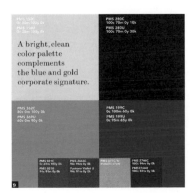

VEHICLES

Tag Line Placement Here
STAPLES

STAPLES
Free Next Day Delivery
Phone # or website

CREDIT CARDS AND SPECIAL PROGRAMS

A common and powerful voice builds confidence that we are experts in our business and that we know our customers' needs. Using the logo correctly reinforces our goal of serving those customers consistently. This is well demonstrated in the application of our identity system to the various credit and promotional program cards. Promoting trust is central to a strong brand. When customers use our credit cards they indicate their trust in our company.

Always use our logo in the upper left corner with the identifier in Senfa Black in the upper right. If implementing a new card program, contact the Manager of Broadcast and Branding.

16 | 17

Client
Washington Mutual Bank
Design Firm
Hornall Anderson Design Works
Designers
John Hornall, Katha Dalton, Holly Finlayson

Don't use the "W" alone.

Client
Western International Media
Design Firm
Glyphix Studio
Designer
Brad Wilder

VISUAL IDENTITY GUIDELINES | WESTERN TYPOGRAPHY

A typeface has been designed exclusively for Western International Media to bring distinctiveness and individuality to collateral material and to complement Western signatures.

The Western Octave typeface is unique to Western International Media. The proprietary typeface is to only be used by approved suppliers who will be responsible for following Western identity guidelines.

Two typeface families can be used withing the Western identity system. These typefaces will be used for headline and text purposes in all Western printed material. They may be used separately or together as appropriate. Never replace Western approved typefaces with alternatives type, not even close substitutes.

Western Octave

ABCDEFGHIJKLM
NOPQRSTUVWXYZ
abcdefghijklmnopqrs
tuvwxyz

Western Octave Regular
Western Octave Bold
Western Octave Italic
WESTERN OCTAVE SMALL CAP

AT Quay Sans (Agfa Type)

ABCDEFGHIJKLM
NOPQRSTUVWXYZ
abcdefghijklmnopq
rstuvwxyz

AT Quay Sans Book
AT Quay Sans Medium

A bright, clean color palette complements the blue and gold corporate signature.

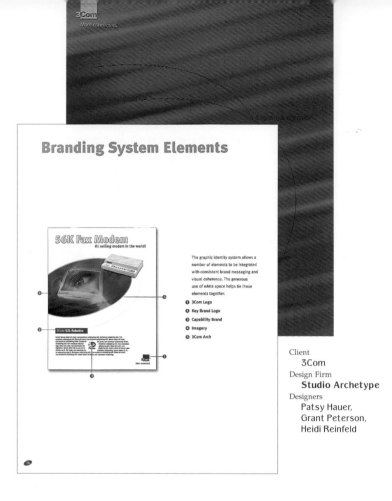

Branding System Elements

The graphic identity system allows a number of elements to be integrated with consistent brand messaging and visual coherence. The generous use of white space helps tie these elements together.

1. 3Com Logo
2. Key Brand Logo
3. Capability Brand
4. Imagery
5. 3Com Arch

Client
3Com
Design Firm
Studio Archetype
Designers
Patsy Hauer,
Grant Peterson,
Heidi Reinfeld

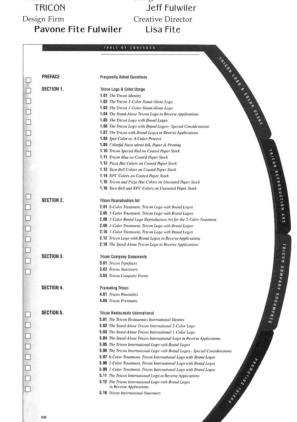

Client
TRICON
Design Firm
Pavone Fite Fulwiler
Designer
Jeff Fulwiler
Creative Director
Lisa Fite

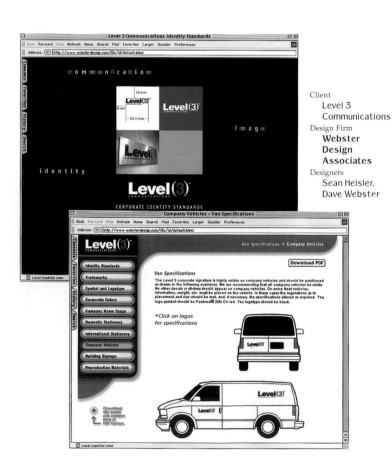

Client
Level 3
Communications
Design Firm
Webster
Design
Associates
Designers
Sean Heisler,
Dave Webster

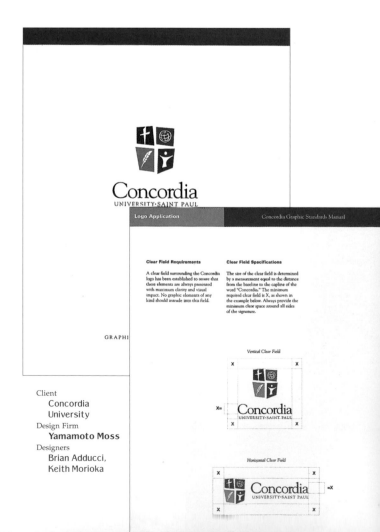

Client
Concordia
University
Design Firm
Yamamoto Moss
Designers
Brian Adducci,
Keith Morioka

Client
  Nicor Inc.
Design Firm
  McMillan Associates
Designer
  Kerri Bautista

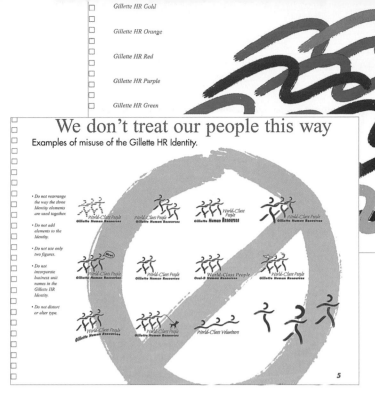

We don't treat our people this way

Examples of misuse of the Gillette HR Identity.

- *Do not rearrange the way the three identity elements are used together.*

- *Do not add elements to the Identity.*

- *Do not use only two figures.*

- *Do not incorporate business unit names in the Gillette HR Identity.*

- *Do not distort or alter type.*

5

Client
  The Gillette Company
Design Firm
  Donaldson Makoski
Designer
  Debby Ryan

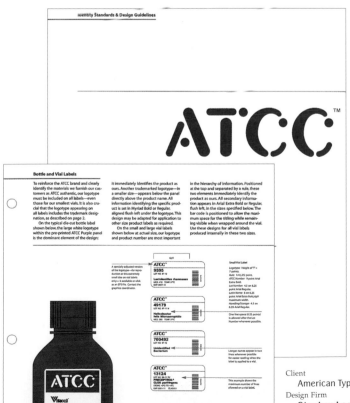

Identity Standards & Design Guidelines

ATCC™

Bottle and Vial Labels

To reinforce the ATCC brand and clearly identify the materials our furnish our customers at ATCC authentic, our logotype must be included on all labels—even those for our smallest vials. It is also crucial that the logotype appearing on all labels includes the trademark designation, as described on page 2.

On the typical die-cut bottle label shown below, the large white logotype within the pre-printed ATCC Purple panel is the dominant element of the design;

it immediately identifies the product as ours. Another trademarked logotype—in a smaller size—appears below the panel directly above the product name. All information identifying the specific product is set in Myriad Bold or Regular, aligned flush left under the logotype. This design may be adapted for application to other size product labels as required.

On the small and large vial labels shown below at actual size, our logotype and product number are most important

in the hierarchy of information. Positioned at the top and separated by a rule, these two elements immediately identify the product as ours. All secondary information appears in Arial Extra Bold or Regular, flush left, in the sizes specified below. The bar code is positioned to allow the maximum space for the titling while remaining visible when wrapped around the vial. Use these designs for all vial labels produced internally in these two sizes.

Client
  American Type Culture Collection
Design Firm
  Stephen Loges Graphic Design
Designer
  Stephen Loges

Client
  Nickelodeon
Design Firm
  The Sloan Group

207

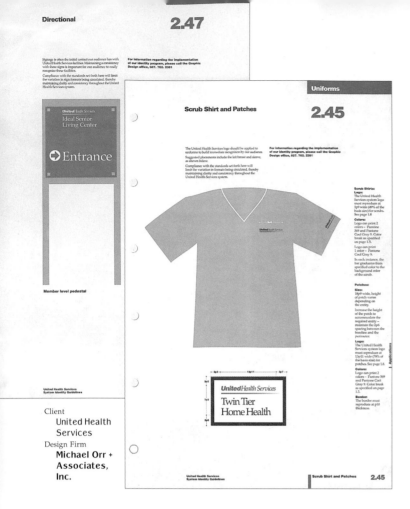

United Health Services
System Identity Guidelines

Client
United Health
Services
Design Firm
**Michael Orr +
Associates,
Inc.**

Client
Royal Caribbean
Design Firm
Yamamoto Moss
Designers
Amanda Groff, Greg Pickman

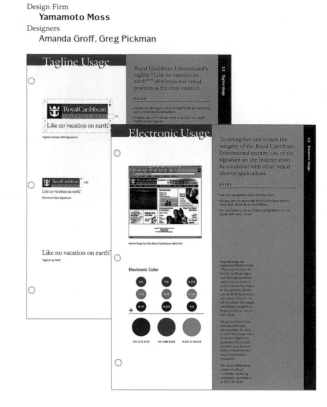

Client
Novartis Crop Protection
Design Firm
Hypermedia Solutions
Designers
Larry Aaron, Jeff O'Donnell

Client
New York University School of Continuing and Professional Studies
Design Firm
O&J Design, Inc.
Designers
Andrzej J. Olejniczak,
Leslie Nayman

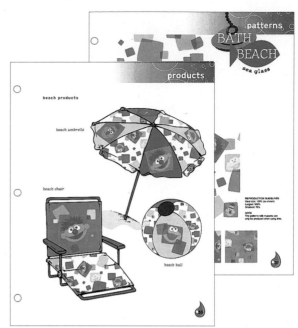

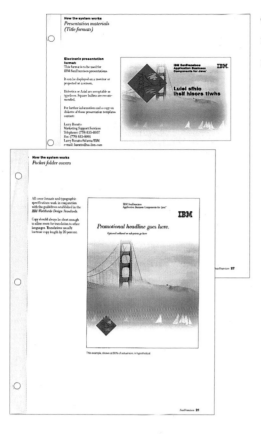

Client
IBM
Design Firm
Ilardi Design
Designers
Salvatore Ilardi,
Jason Nocera

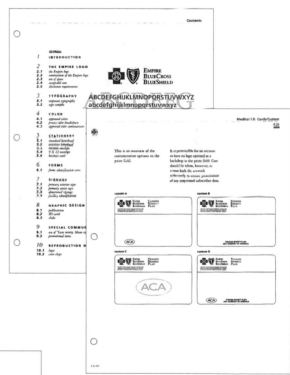

Client
Children's Television
Workshop
Design Firm
The Sloan Group
Designer
Rachel Ericson
Art Director
Rita Arifin

Client
Empire Blue Cross Blue Shield
Design Firm
Handler Design Group
Designers
John Ryan, Bruce Handler

Client
Anacomp
Design Firm
Mires Design
Designer
Deborah Hom
Art Director
John Ball
Illustrator
Miguel Perez

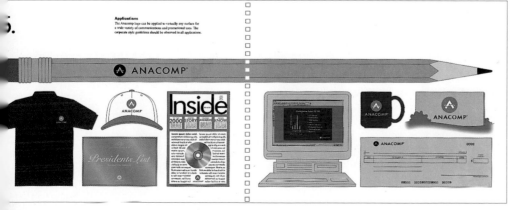

Signage & Environmental Graphics

Client
  PB&J Restaurants/Yahooz
  Contemporary Cowboy Cuisiune
Design Firm
  EAT Advertising & Design, Inc.
Designers
  Patrice Eilts-Jobe, Jeff Miller

Client
  Disney Cruise Line
Design Firm
  David Carter Design Assoc.
Creative Director
  Lori B. Wilson
Designer
  Cynthia Carter

Client
  Lifetime Television
Design Firm
  Lorenc Design
Designers
  Jan Lorenc,
  Steve McCall

Client
  Hilton
Design Firm
  Schafer

Client
    GES Exposition Services
Design Firm
    Tieken Design & Creative Services
Designer
    Fred E. Tieken

Client
    Donut King
Design Firm
    Lorenc Design
Designers
    Jan Lorenc,
    Chung Youl Yoo

Client
    FOX Sports Direct
Design Firm
    Swieter Design U.S.
Designers
    John Swieter, Mark Ford,
    Cameron Smith,
    Carlos Perez, Julie Poth

Client
    Georgia Pacific
Design Firm
    Lorenc Design
Designers
    Jan Lorenc, John Lauer,
    Rory Myers

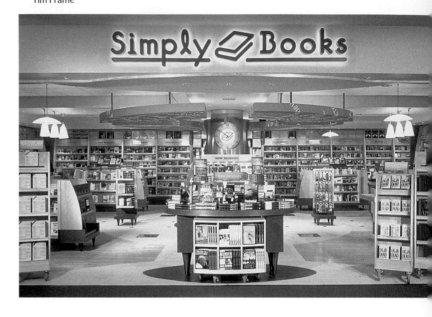

Client
KIVA
Design Firm
Chute Gerdeman, Inc.
Designers
Susan Hessler, Adam Limbach

Client
Gerber Scientific
Design Firm
Donaldson Makoski
Designer
Debby Ryan

Client
Donatos Pizza
Design Firm
Chute Gerdeman, Inc.
Designer
Adam Limbach

Client
Georgia Center for Children
Design Firm
Lorenc Design
Designers
Jan Lorenc, David Park

213

Client
    Dick's Clothing & Sporting Goods
Design Firm
    FRCH Design Worldwide
Designers
    Niki Adrian, Paul Lechleiter

Client
    79 North Industrial Park
Design Firm
    Agnew Moyer Smith Inc.
Designer
    Norm Goldberg

Client
    Hyatt
Design Firm
    FRCH Design Worldwide
Designers
    Gary Cieradkowski,
    John Kennedy

Client
    Paramount Group Inc.
Design Firm
    FRCH Design Worldwide
Designers
    Ray Berberich, Michael Beeghly,
    Sandra Pancoe, Trish Baum

Client
Landau & Heyman
Design Firm
T L Horton Design
Principal
Tony Horton

Client
Toscano Ristorante
Design Firm
Sayles Graphic Design
Designer
John Sayles

Client
Ripley's Aquariums
Design Firm
JGA, Inc.
Designer
Brian Eastman

Client
Pennsylvania Fashions
Design Firm
JGA, Inc.
Designers
Tony Camilletti, Michael Farris

Client
Digital Output
Design Firm
Visual Asylum
Designers
Amy Jo Levine,
MaeLin Levine

Client
Zehnder's Marketplace
Design Firm
JGA, Inc.
Designer
Brian Eastman

Client
Centre City Development Corporation,
City of San Diego
Design Firm
Nicholson Design
Designers
Joe C. Nicholson

Client
Trans World Dome & St. Louis Rams
Design Firm
Kiku Obata & Company
Designers
Scott Gericke, Russell Buchanan, Jr.,
Nao Etsuki, Jonathan Bryant, Heather Testa

Client
   St. Louis Children's Zoo
Design Firm
   Kiku Obata & Company
Principal
   Kiku Obata, Todd Mayberry, Rich Nelson,
   Arden Powell, Jonathan Bryant

Client
   The Museums at 18th and Vine
Design Firm
   Kiku Obata & Company
Designer
   Kiku Obata, Chris Mueller, Rich Nelson,
   Al Sacui, Tim McGinty, Gen Obata, Heather Testa

Client
   Discovery Communications, Inc.
Design Firm
   Discovery Design Group
Designer
   Bill Buttaggi
Art Director
   Janet Daniel

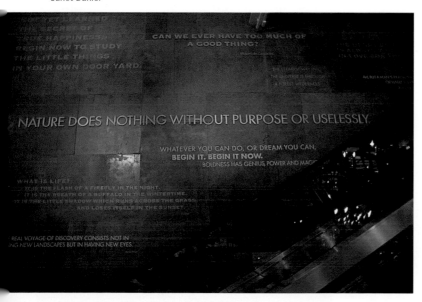

Client
   BJC Health Systems &
   Washington University Medical Center
Design Firm
   Kiku Obata & Company
Designers
   Kiku Obata, Rich Nelson, Todd Mayberry,
   Teresa Norton-Young, Russell Buchanan, Jr.,
   Tim Wheeler, Carole Jerome

Client
   Pittsburgh Auditorium Authority
Design Firm
   Neoforma Design & Mavrovic Architects
Designers
   Paul Borrero, Michelle Lee

Client
   Guess? Inc.
Design Firm
   Desgrippes Gobe
Designer
   Victoria Kirk, Mark Oller

Client
   The Muny Theater of St. Louis
Design Firm
   Kiku Obata & Company
Designers
   Todd Mayberry, Gen Obata, Jonathan Bryant

Client
   Silver Legacy Casino
Design Firm
   David Carter Design Assoc.
Designers
   David Carter Design Assoc.

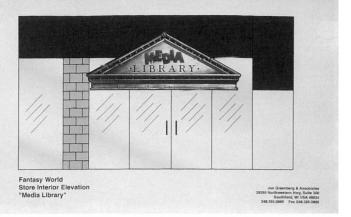

Fantasy World
Store Interior Elevation
"Media Library"

Jon Greenberg & Associates
29355 Northwestern Hwy, Suite 300
Southfield, MI USA 48034
248.355.0890 Fax 248.355.0895

Client
   Fantasy World
Design Firm
   JGA, Inc.
Designer
   Brian Eastman

Client
   Discovery Communications Inc.
Design Firm
   Discovery Design Group
Designer
   Stefan Poulos
Art Director
   Janet Daniel

Client
   Pepsico Restaurants International
Design Firm
   Design Continuum Inc.
Designers
   Jane Hathaway, Claire Bowen, Richard Davia

Client
   Discovery Communications Inc.
Design Firm
   Discovery Design Group
Designer
   Bill Buttaggi
Art Director
   Janet Daniel

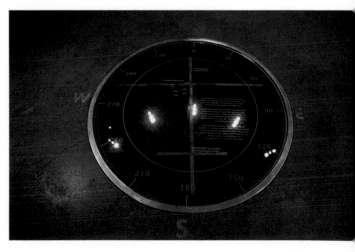

Corporate Image Brochures

Client
Phoenix Creative
Design Firm
Phoenix Creative, St. Louis
Designer
Ed Mantels-Seeker

Client
Rosewood Hotels & Resorts
Design Firm
David Carter Design Associates
Designer
Sharon Le Jeune
Creative Director
Lori B. Wilson

Client
Target Stores
Design Firm
Design Guys
Designer
Dawn Selg

Client
HDS Processors
Design Firm
HDS Marcomm
Designer
Gayle T. Ono

Client
Guadalupe Alternative Programs
Design Firm
Franke + Fiorella
Designer
Kathy Lambert

Client
    Mohawk Paper Mills
Design Firm
    Hornall Anderson Design Works
Designers
    Jack Anderson, Lisa Cerveny,
    Mary Hermes, Jana Nishi,
    Jana Wilson Esser, Virginia Le

Client
    The Metropolitan Museum of Art
Design Firm
    The Valentine Group
Designers
    Robert Valentine, Stephanie Relkin

Client
    Star Corrugated
Design Firm
    Studio Morris LA/NY
Designers
    Jeffrey Morris, Susan Moriguchi

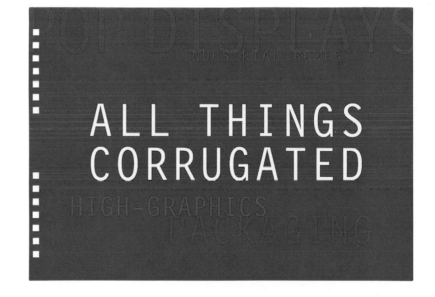

Client
    Informatics Studio, Inc.
Design Firm
    Informatics Studio, Inc.
Designers
    Wendy Garfinkel, Todd Cavalier

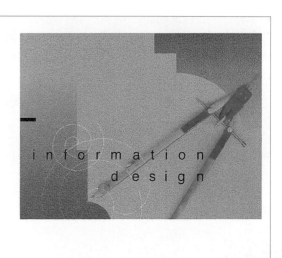

Client
   Phoenix Creative
Design Firm
   **Phoenix Creative,
   St. Louis**
Designer
   Ed Mantels-Seeker

Client
   Boy Scouts of America
Design Firm
   Duke Marketing Communications
Designers
   Justin Ahrens, Chad Nelson

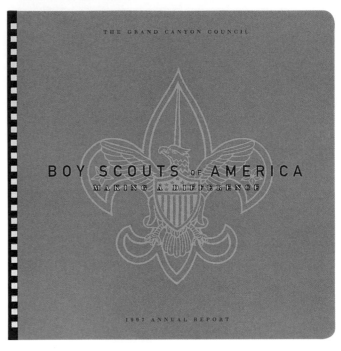

Client
   Magna Bank
Design Firm
   Bartels & Company
Designer
   David Bartels, Ron Rodemacher

Client
   Dharma
Design Firm
   Susan Bercu Design Studio
Designer
   Susan Bercu

Client
The Richard E. Jacobs Group
Design Firm
Herip Associates
Designers
Walter M. Herip, John R. Menter

Client
Commonwealth of Pennsylvania
Design Firm
A to Z communications, inc.
Designer
Ed Sutton

Client
Wallace/Church
Design Firm
Wallace/Church
Designers
Stan Church, Andrew Cawrse

Client
Mars 2112
Design Firm
Daroff Design Inc
Designers
Glenn Swantak,
Simone Makoul,
Jack Hulme

223

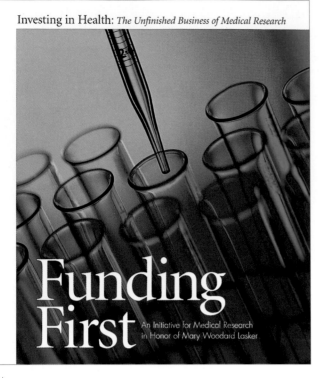

Investing in Health: The Unfinished Business of Medical Research

Funding First

An Initiative for Medical Research in Honor of Mary Woodard Lasker

Client
Mary Woodward Lasker Charitable Trust
Design Firm
AXIS Communications
Designer
Tamara Dowd

Client
Crown Floorcovering
Design Firm
Design Room
Designer
Chad Gordon

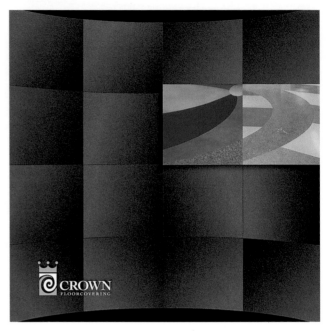

What kind *of grade would* Perspectives *give itself?*

¿Qué nota se daría
Perspectives por su actuación?

A report on the
1997-98 school year
— and a look ahead.

Un informe del año
escolar 1997-98...
y una mirada hacia
el futuro.

Client
Perspectives Charter School
Design Firm
Design Kitchen Inc.
Designer
Andy Keene

Client
UIS, Inc.
Design Firm
Tom Fowler, Inc.
Designer
Karl S. Maruyama

Client
  IDETIX
Design Firm
  FCS
Designers
  Jackie Green, Frank Fisher

Vitrix Hot Glass Studio

Client
  Vitrix Hot Glass Studio
Design Firm
  Michael Orr + Associates, Inc.
Designers
  Michael R. Orr, Thomas Freeland

Client
  Franke + Fiorella
Design Firm
  Franke + Fiorella
Designer
  Craig Franke

Client
  Color Dynamics
Design Firm
  David Carter Design
Designer
  Emily Cain
Creative Director
  Lori B. Wilson

225

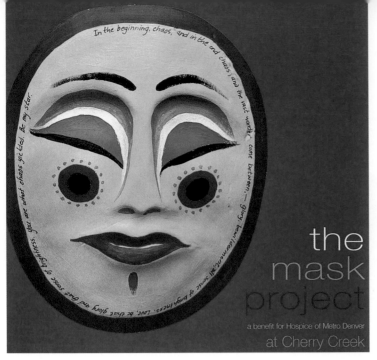

In the beginning, chaos, and in the end chaos; and the rest work; come between—glory brightness. you are what chaos yielded. Be my star.

the
mask
project
a benefit for Hospice of Metro Denver
at Cherry Creek

Client
Cherry Creek Shopping Center
Design Firm
Ellen Bruss Design
Designers
Ellen Bruss, Charles Carpenter, Greg Carr

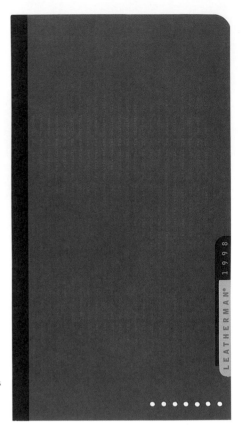

Client
Leatherman Tool Group
Design Firm
Hornall Anderson Design Works
Designers
Jack Anderson, Lisa Cerveny,
David Bates

PREMIUM HANDMADE CIGARS

U.S. CIGAR
QUALITY AND CRAFTSMANSHIP
Dominican Republic, Honduras

Client
U.S. Cigar
Design Firm
**Hornall Anderson
Design Works**
Designers
Jack Anderson,
Larry Anderson,
Mary Hermes,
Mike Calkins,
David Bates,
Michael Brugman

Client
The Gunlocke Company
Design Firm
Michael Orr + Associates, Inc.
Designers
Michael R. Orr, Thomas Freeland

226

Client
    Seasonal Specialties LLC
Design Firm
    Seasonal Specialties In House Creative
Designers
    Jennifer Sheeler, Barbara J. Roth, Lisa Milan
Production
    Deborah Lee, Rene Demel, Larisa Gieneart

Client
    La Mansion del Rio
Design Firm
    David Carter Design Assoc.
Designer
    Katherine Baronet
Creative Director
    Lori B. Wilson

Client
    Liz J. Design
Design Firm
    Liz J. Design

Client
    Creative Fusions
Design Firm
    Tim Girvin Design, Inc.
Designer
    Kim Edberg

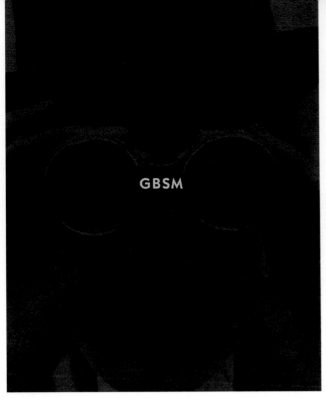

Client
GBSM
Design Firm
Rassman Design
Designers
John Rassman, Amy Rassman,
Lyn D'Amato, Vicki Freeman

Client
Houlihan Lokey
Howard & Zukin
Design Firm
Julia Tam Design
Designer
Julia Tam

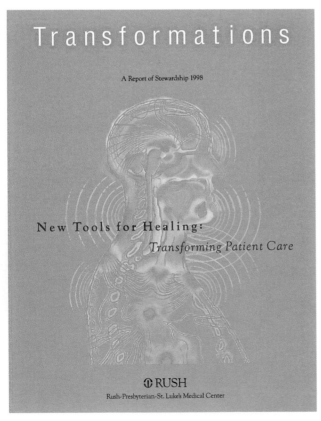

Client
Rush Presbyterian
—St. Luke's
Design Firm
Brierton Design
Designers
Michael Brierton,
Kirk Hitschel,
Martin Cimek

Client
Blackboard
Design Firm
Elliott Van Deutsch
Designers
Rachel Deutsch,
Ann Lesch,
Tom Cosgrave

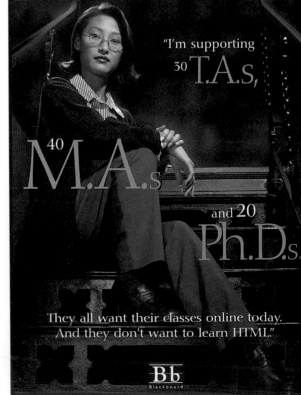

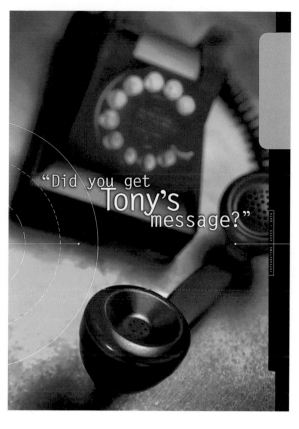

Client
    General Magic
Design Firm
    Hornall Anderson
    Design Works
Designers
    Jack Anderson,
    Jana Nishi,
    Mary Chin Hutchison,
    Mike Brugman

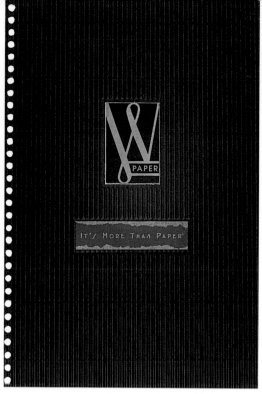

Client
    Wisconsin Paper Co.
Design Firm
    Z · D Studios, Inc.
Designer
    Mark W. Schmitz

Client
    Crown Construction
Design Firm
    Jasper & Bridge
Designer
    Andy Thorington

Client
    Taylor Made Golf
Design Firm
    Laura Coe
    Design Associates
Designers
    Laura Coe Wright,
    Denise Heisey

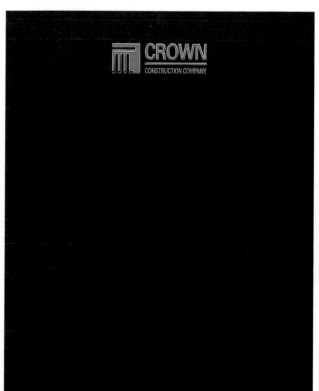

Client
   Mahlum
Design Firm
   Hornall Anderson Design Works
Designers
   Jack Anderson, Heidi Favour,
   Bruce Branson-Meyer, Mary Hermes

Client
   Natural Resource Group, Inc.
Design Firm
   Lynn Schulte Design
Designer
   Lynn Schulte
Copywriter
   Dan Wallace

Client
   Creative Show of San Diego
Design Firm
   Visual Asylum
Designers
   Amy Jo Levine, MaeLin Levine, Joel Sotelo

Client
   Tarmac Demaco Block
Design Firm
   CadmusCom
Designer
   Susan M. Walsh

Client
St. Patrick Center
Design Firm
Bartels & Company
Designers
David Bartels, Ron Rodemacher

Client
Georgia-Pacific Corp.
Design Firm
Leslie Evans Design Associates
Designers
Leslie Evans, Teresa Cummings, Cheri Bryant

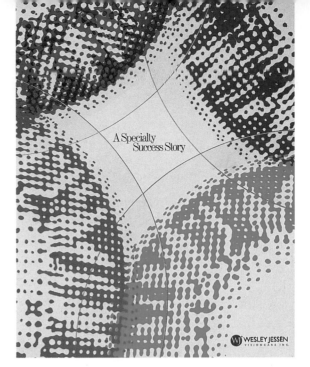

Client
Wesley Jessen
Design Firm
Crowley Webb & Associates
Designer
Dion Pender

Client
Palm West Golf
Design Firm
Duke Marketing Communications
Designers
Justin Ahrens, Chad Nelson

231

AND IT SHOWS IN THE

We'll let the critics speak for themselves:

CRITICAL ACCLAIM

"In the 15 years that HBO has been in

the filmmaking business, it has carved

out a reputation for doing movies better

than anyone in TV. That's not opinion.

That's fact." —*Variety, November 9, 1997*

Client
HBO
Design Firm
The Sloan Group
Director
Heather Baris

Client
Delta V Technologies, Inc.
Design Firm
Boelts Bros. Associates
Designers
Jackson Boelts, Kerry Stratford, Elicia Taylor

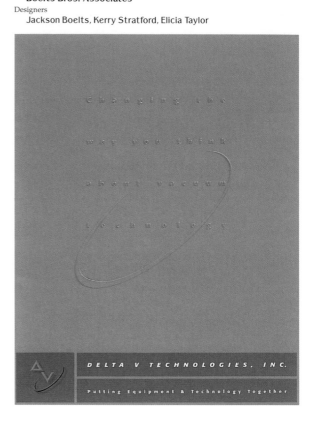

Client
Sprig Circuits
Design Firm
Bau Mac Communications
Designer
Tara Baumann

Client
Lee Company
Design Firm
**Willoughby
Design Group**
Designer
Ingred Sidie

232

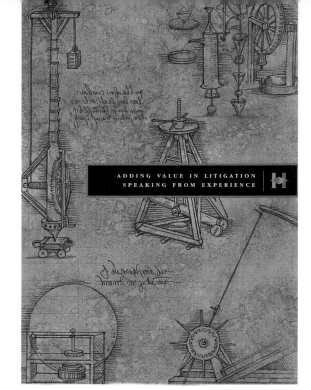

Client
Houlihan Lokey Howard & Zukin
Design Firm
Julia Tam Design
Designer
Julia Tam

Client
Rex Healthcare
Design Firm
**Peter Taflan Marketing
Communications, Inc.**
Designers
Jacque Taylor, Stan Elder,
Janssen Strother

Client
CSC
Design Firm
Ramona Hutko Design
Designer
Ramona Hutko

Client
IBM
Design Firm
Doyle Partners
Creative Director, Designer
Stephen Doyle
Photographer
Victor Schrager

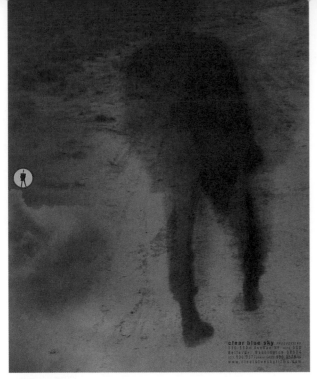

Client
    Clear Blue Sky Productions
Design Firm
    Werkhaus Design
Designer
    Christina Stein

Client
    Rose Manufacturing
Design Firm
    **A to Z
    communications, inc.**
Designer
    Aimee Lazer

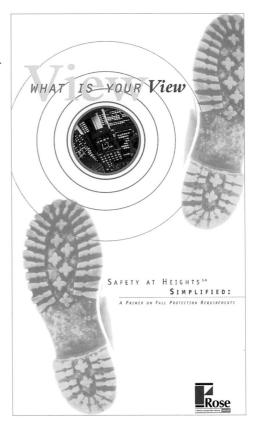

Client
    Love Packaging Group
Design Firm
    Love Packaging Group
Designer
    Chris West

Client
    The Winter Construction Company
Design Firm
    B-man Design
Designer
    Barry Brager

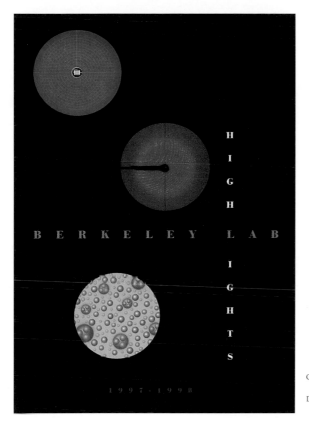

Client
  Berkeley Lab
Design Firm
  Niza Hanany/Public Information Dept.

Client
  Tom Dolle Design
Design Firm
  Tom Dolle Design
Designers
  Tom Dolle, Chris Riely

Client
  Dermalogica
Design Firm
  BRD Design
Designer
  Matthias Mencke

Client
  Yamamoto Moss
Design Firm
  Yamamoto Moss
Designers
  Gretchen Blase,
  Hideki Yamamoto

Client
RH Donnelley
Design Firm
**Marjorie Gross + Company/
Tom Dolle Design**
Designers
Tom Dolle, Chris Riely

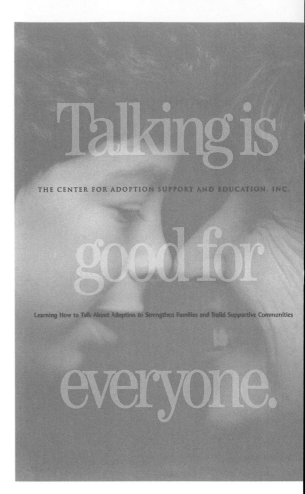

Client
Alphabet Soup
Design Firm
**Sayles
Graphic Design**
Designer
John Sayles

Client
CASE Center for Adoption Support and Education
Design Firm
AXIS Communications
Designer
Tamara Dowd, Craig Byers

Client
Hotel Pattee
Design Firm
Sayles Graphic Design
Designer
John Sayles

Client
Interface
Design Firm
The Valentine Group
Designers
Jin Chung,
Stephanie Relkin
Creative Director
Robert Valentine

Client
Prometheus Network Solutions
Design Firm
Oxygen, Inc.
Designers
Penina Goodman, Michelle Goldish

Client
Equinox
Design Firm
Wechsler Ross & Partners Inc.
Senior Designer
Amber de Janosi
Design Director
Stephen Visconti

Client
CadmusCom
Design Firm
CadmusCom
Designer
Cathy Oliver

Client
Ogilvy & Mather
Design Firm
O & J Design Inc.
Designers
Andrzej J. Olejniczak,
Christina Mueller

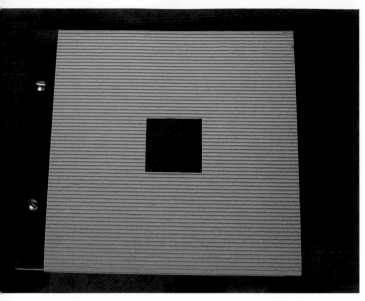

Client
Discovery Communications
Design Firm
Discovery Design Group
Designer
Janet Daniel

Client
U.S. Cigar
Design Firm
Hornall Anderson Design Works
Designers
Jack Anderson, Mary Hermes, Larry Anderson,
Mike Calkins, David Bates, Michael Brugman

Client
Galileo International
Design Firm
Sayles Graphic Design
Designer
John Sayles

Client
Zunda Design Group
Design Firm
Zunda Design Group
Designer
Charles Zunda,
Todd Nickel, Jon Voss

Client
La Crosse County
Solid Waste Disposal System
Design Firm
Foth & Van Dyke
Designer
Daniel Green

Client
DAM Creative
Design Firm
Kendall Creative Shop
Designer
Mark K. Platt

Client
Hadassah Convention
Department
Design Firm
Hadassah Creative Services
Designer
Irit Hadari
Art Director
Michael Cohen

Client
The Cooper Union for the
Advancement of Science & Art
Design Firm
Drive Communications
Designer
Michael Graziolo

Client
Memphis Redbirds
Design Firm
Thompson & Company
Designers
Trace Hallowell,
David Steinke

239

Client
Good Dog Advertising
Design Firm
Sweiter Design U.S.
Designer
Julie Poth

Client
BBDLLC
Design Firm
Greg Welsh Design
Designer
Greg Welsh

Client
HTML Compendium
Designer
Leo Kopelow

Client
Colorbus
Design Firm
McAdams Group
Designer
Randy Nickle

Client
Ford Motor Co.
Design Firm
**Ervin Marketing
Creative Communications**
Designer
Erica Schwan

Client
Environmental Council
of the University of Illinois
Design Firm
Clarke Communication Design
Designer
John V. Clarke

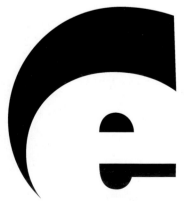

Client
Northern Virginia Science
& Technology Center
Design Firm
neo design
Designer
DJ Min

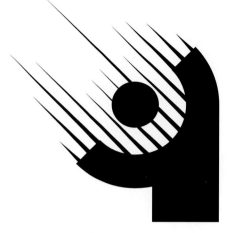

Client
SWD Holding's, Inc.
Design Firm
Gauger & Silva
Designer
Lori Murphy

Client
The Spring Garden
Design Firm
Crowley Webb & Associates
Designer
Brian Grunert

Client
Ecker Enterprises
Design Firm
WATCH! Graphic Design
Designer
Bruno Watel

Client
Dever Designs
Design Firm
Dever Designs
Designer
Jeffrey L. Dever

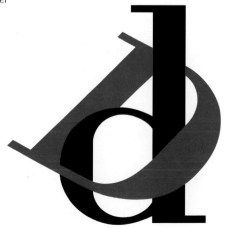

Client
Ford Motor Co.
Design Firm
Ervin Marketing
Creative Communications
Designer
Erica Schwan

Client
    Sheffield Pharmaceuticals, Inc.
Design Firm
    Crowley Webb & Associates
Designer
    Dion Pender

Client
    Peninsula Foods, Inc.
Design Firm
    The Visual Group
Designer
    Ark Stein

Client
    Nike Inc.
Design Firm
    Mires Design
Designers
    John Ball,
    Miguel Perez

Client
    Groft Design
Design Firm
    Groft Design
Designer
    Randy Groft

Client
    Awear Inc.
Design Firm
    Nicholas Associates/Chicago
Designers
    Nick Sinadinos,
    Scott Hardy

Client
    Technology Square
Design Firm
    Sasaki Associates
Designers
    Kris Waldman,
    Leslie Jonas

Client
Oak River Financial Group, Inc.
Design Firm
Michael Lee Advertising
& Design, Inc.
Designers
Michael Lee,
Debby Stasinopoulou

Client
Two Trees Technologies
Design Firm
Walsh Associates
Designer
Dan Van Buskirk

Client
Color Image
Graphic & Printing
Design Firm
Imtech Communications
Designer
Robert Keng

Client
Buckhead Life
Restaurant Group
Design Firm
Rousso + Associates
Designer
Steve Rousso

Client
Broudy Printing Inc.
Design Firm
Lamfers & Associates
Designers
Missy Nery,
Debra Lamfers

Broudy Printing Inc.
SEE THE POWER OF FINE PRINTING

Client
Sapient Corporation
Design Firm
Gill Fishman Assoc., Inc.
Designer
Michael Persons

Client
  Wearhouse
Design Firm
  Georgopulos Design
Designer
  Jonathan Georgopulos

Client
  Wester Landscape Management
Design Firm
  Michael Lee Advertising & Design, Inc.
Designer
  Michael Lee

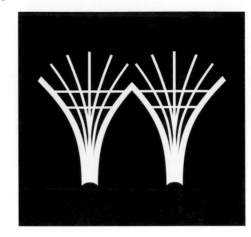

Client
  Nabisco
Design Firm
  Hans Flink Design Inc.
Designer
  Mike Troian

Client
  Microtech Systems
Design Firm
  The Visual Group
Designer
  Ark Stein

Client
  Colgate Palmolive Co.
Design Firm
  Hans Flink Design Inc.
Designers
  Mark Krukonis,
  Mike Troian

Client
  Capstone Advisors
Design Firm
  Ford & Earl Associates
Designer
  Todd Malhoit

244

Client
Small Valve Payments Co.
Design Firm
Rowe & Ballantine
Designers
Edward Rowe,
John Baccantine

Client
Los Angeles Firemen's Credit Union
Design Firm
The Rakela Company
Designer
Douglas Deibel

Client
Synergy
Design Firm
Artemis Creative, Inc.
Designers
Wes Aoki,
Gary Nusinow,
Ian Smith

Client
Unilever HPC
Design Firm
Hans Flink Design Inc.
Designers
Susan Kunschaft,
Chang Mei Lin

Client
Brand Space
Design Firm
Emmerling Post, Inc.
Designer
Stuart Cohen

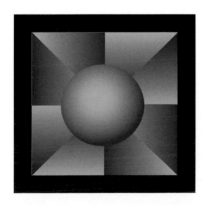

BRANDSPACE™

Client
Otay Ranch
Design Firm
Tyler Blik Design
Designers
Tracy Sabin,
Ron Fleming

Client
  Waterspoint Lake
Design Firm
  Miller & White Advertising
Designers
  Brian Miller,
  Brad Goodwin

Client
  Software Solutions
Design Firm
  Rousso + Associates
Designer
  Steve Rousso

Client
  Brent Humphries, Photographer
Design Firm
  Swieter Design U.S.
Designer
  Mark Ford

Client
  Mode Magazine
Design Firm
  360°, Inc.
Designers
  Herta Kriegner,
  Janine Weitenauer,
  Tim Hossler

Client
  Double Take
Design Firm
  Hedstrom/Blessing
Designer
  Wendy LaBreche

Client
  DAM Creative
Design Firm
  Kendall Creative Shop
Designer
  Mark K. Platt

246

Client
Charger Electric Bikes
Design Firm
Swieter Design U.S.
Designer
John Swieter

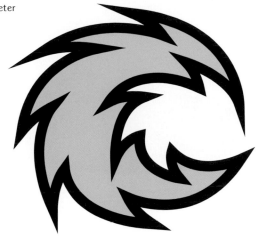

Client
Camp Max Straus Foundation
Design Firm
Davies Associates
Designers
Cathy Davies,
Omar Noorzay

Client
Eminent Research Systems
Design Firm
ZGraphics, Ltd.
Designers
Renee Clark,
Joe Zeller

Client
Dennis Murphy Photography
Design Firm
Swieter Design U.S.
Designers
Dennis Murphy,
Cameron Smith

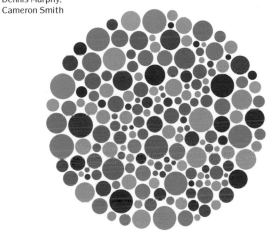

Client
Teplick Laser Surgery Centers
Design Firm
Woodson & Newroth
Designer
Ken Steckler

Client
Kaufmann Management Group
Design Firm
Ogilvy and Mather/Houston
Designer
Greg Kewekordes

Client
Sierra Pacific Constructors, Inc.
Design Firm
Davies Associates
Designers
Cathy Davies,
Omar Noorzay

Client
Coolsville Records
Design Firm
Michael Doret Graphic Design
Designer
Michael Doret

Client
Dell Computer Corporation
Design Firm
EHR Design
Designer
Carlos Zapata

Client
Piatti Restaurant Company
Design Firm
Hunt Weber Clark Associates
Designer
Leigh Krichbaum

Client
Infinet Incorporated
Design Firm
Cathey Associates, Inc.
Designer
Gordon Cathey

Client
Star Trac
Design Firm
RiechesBaird
Designer
Masa Lau

Client
    Classified Ventures
Design Firm
    Swieter Design U.S.
Designer
    Mark Ford

Client
    Belyea
Design Firm
    Belyea
Designer
    Ron Lars Hansen

Client
    Cañon Swim & Tennis Club
Design Firm
    Triad, Inc.
Designer
    Diana Kollanyi

Client
    Cleveland Zoological Society
Design Firm
    Nesnadny + Schwartz
Designer
    Timothy Lachina

Client
    European Attic
Design Firm
    Walsh Associates
Designer
    Kerry Walsh

Client
    Akropolis Network
Design Firm
    Design Goes Inc.
Designer
    Robert Goes

Client
Fenton Hill Florida
Design Firm
Chute Gerdeman, Inc.
Designer
Alan Jazak

Client
Leeann Chin
Design Firm
Foley Sackett
Designer
Chris Cortilet

Client
Edison International
Design Firm
Perceive
Designer
Jamie Graupner

Client
GSH Design
Design Firm
Design Lab
Designer
Kennah Harcum

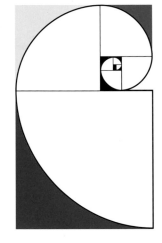

Client
WoodTrader
Design Firm
Nesnadny + Schwartz
Designers
Timothy Lachina,
Gregory Oznowich,
Brian Lavy

Client
Seattle Aquarium
Design Firm
The Leonhardt Group
Designer
Thad Boss

Client
  Boston Stock Exchange
Design Firm
  Gill Fishman Assoc., Inc.
Designer
  Alicia Stephenson

Client
  Netcom On-Line
  Communication Services
Design Firm
  Landkamer Partners
Designers
  Gene Clark,
  Mark Landkamer

BOSTON
STOCK EXCHANGE

Client
  Crossey Engineering
Design Firm
  Nesnadny + Schwartz
Designer
  Joyce Nesnadny

Client
  IVS, Avstar Automotive
  Navigation System
Design Firm
  Perceive
Designer
  Jamie Graupner

Client
  Expeditor's International
Design Firm
  The Leonhardt Group
Designers
  Tim Young,
  Janee Kreinleder

Client
  Alpine Lodging
Design Firm
  Art 270, Inc.
Designers
  John Opet,
  Carl Mill

TRADEWIN™

ALPINE
LODGING

TELLURIDE

Client
  Hunter Douglas Wood Products
Design Firm
  Tieken Design &
  Creative Services
Designer
  Fred E. Tieken

Client
  Hausman Design, Inc.
Design Firm
  Hausman Design, Inc.
Designers
  Linda Aryani,
  Joan L. Hausman

Client
  Pacific Design Center
Design Firm
  Lane + Lane
Designers
  Brian Lane,
  Tracey Lane

Client
  Lumature
Design Firm
  Tieken Design &
  Creative Services
Designers
  Rik Boberg,
  Fred E. Tieken

Client
  Dan Corbin & Associates
Design Firm
  Artworks
Designer
  Clifford Fudge

Client
  Excidian
Design Firm
  Informatics Studio, Inc.
Designers
  Wendy Garfinkel,
  Todd Cavalier,
  Radoj Glisic

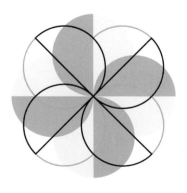

Client
Simplify
Design Firm
Wechsler Ross & Partners
Designers
Karen Knorr,
Cherese Rambaldi

Client
PhotosOnCD
Design Firm
**Tieken Design &
Creative Services**
Designer
Fred E. Tieken

simplify

PHOTOSON**CD**

Client
Art Plus Technology
Design Firm
Art Plus Technology
Designers
Gary Clark,
Robert Linisky

Client
Olympic Pools
Design Firm
RMorris Design
Designer
Rock Morris

apt art plus technology for business^{SM}

Client
Infoseek
Design Firm
Studio Archetype
Designers
Grant Peterson,
Bob Skubik,
Tom Gehring

Client
Rabbit Fest
Design Firm
Rabbit Fest Logo
Designer
Keith Dotson

Rabbit
F·E·S·T

Client
    Convergent Networks
Design Firm
    Partners & Simons
Designer
    Karen Zraket

Client
    Vital Images
Design Firm
    Foley Sackett
Designer
    Chris Cortilet

Convergent Networks

Client
    max.mobil
Design Firm
    Straightline International
Designer
    Ivo Waldburger

Client
    Encore Acquisition (Oil & Gas)
Design Firm
    Graphic Concepts Group
Designer
    Bill Buck

Client
    Feld Entertainment
Design Firm
    Capstone Studios, Inc.
Designers
    JoAnne Redwood,
    John Dismukes

Client
    Extricity Software
Design Firm
    1185 Design
Designers
    Julia Foug,
    Peggy Burke

Client
  Precision Response Corporation
Design Firm
  BarretLaidlawGervais
Designer
  David Laidlaw

Client
  Holocomm Systems, Inc.
Design Firm
  Lorenz Advertising & Design
Designer
  Arne Ratermanis

Client
  Dundee Main Street
Design Firm
  ZGraphics, Ltd.
Designers
  Gregg Rojewski,
  Joe Zeller

Client
  Ignition
Design Firm
  latitude
Designer
  Rob Johnson

Client
  Western International Media
Design Firm
  Glyphix Studio
Designer
  Brad Wilder

Client
  Epic Megagames
Design Firm
  Capstone Studios, Inc.
Designer
  John Taylor Dismukes

WESTERN INTERNATIONAL MEDIA

Client
  Phoenix Education Summit
Design Firm
  Designkit, Inc.
Designers
  Kelly Quashnie,
  Kit Örn

Client
  Your Money
  "Consumer's Digest"
Design Firm
  Capstone Studios, Inc.
Designers
  JoAnne Redwood,
  John Dismukes

Client
  The Marks Brothers
Design Firm
  Nicholas Associates/Chicago
Designers
  Nick Sinadinos,
  Melissa Hersam

THE MA®KS BROTHERS

Client
  C. J. Woodmaster
Design Firm
  **Peter Taflan Marketing
  Communications, Inc.**
Designer
  Janssen Strother

Client
  Point & Click, Inc.
Design Firm
  Drive Communications
Designer
  Michael Graziolo

Point & Click

Client
  Sendmail, Inc.
Design Firm
  Profile Design
Designers
  Tony Meador,
  Joanna Dolby,
  Michael Fu-Ming

SENDMAIL

Client
  DeStefano/Hrones
Design Firm
  WATCH! Graphic Design
Designer
  Bruno Watel

Client
  Lexington Memorial Hospital
Design Firm
  **Peter Taflan Marketing
  Communications, Inc.**
Designer
  Janssen Strother

Client
  Technicolor
Design Firm
  **Tsuchiya Sloneker
  Communications**
Designer
  Matthew Schneider

Client
  Advantagekbs
Design Firm
  David Morris Creative Inc.
Designer
  Glenn Gontha

Client
  ProSourcing
Design Firm
  Fuller Designs, Inc.
Designer
  Doug Fuller

Client
  Kiva
Design Firm
  Chute Gerdeman, Inc.
Designers
  Susan Hessler,
  Adam Limbach

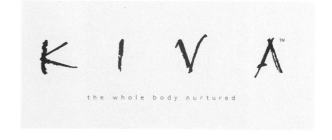

Client
  Alpine Lodging
Design Firm
  Art 270, Inc.
Designers
  Pat Singer,
  Carl Mill

ALPINE LODGING

T E L L U R I D E

Client
  Richter Systems
Design Firm
  California Design Int'l
Designers
  Chris Ardito,
  Chuck Long,
  Dan Liew

Client
  Proxenus Game Improvement Systems
Design Firm
  Groft Design
Designer
  Randy Groft

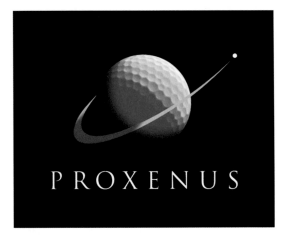

PROXENUS

Client
  Hyperion Solutions Corporation
Design Firm
  Landkamer Partners
Designers
  Gene Clark,
  Mark Landkamer

HYPERiON®

Client
  Office of National Drug Control Policy
Design Firm
  Crosby Associates Inc.
Designer
  Bart Crosby

Project k**NO**w for drug education and prevention.

Client
  Ideam
Design Firm
  Giordano Kearfott Design
Designers
  Susan Giordano,
  Lee Ater

258

Client
Creative Fusions
Design Firm
Tim Girvin Design, Inc.
Designer
Kim Edberg

Client
Eagle Crest Shoes + Boots
Design Firm
Art 270, Inc.
Designers
Steve Kuttruff,
Carl Mill

Client
California Sciencenter
Design Firm
Nicholas Associates/Chicago
Designer
Nick Sinadinos

Client
McMillian Design
Design Firm
McMillian Design
Designer
William McMillian

Client
Epigram
Design Firm
Landkamer Partners
Designers
Gene Clark,
Mark Landkamer

Client
Big Flower Press
Design Firm
Susan Hochbaum Design
Designer
Susan Hochbaum

Client
City of Chicago
Design Firm
Crosby Associates Inc.
Designer
Bart Crosby

Client
Bernard Zell Anshe Emet Day School
Design Firm
Crosby Associates Inc.
Designer
Bart Crosby

Chicago2001

For the time of your life.

Bernard Zell Anshe Emet Day School
1998 Holiday Shopping Festival

Client
Jamestown Packaging
Design Firm
Edward Walter Design
Designer
Edward Walter

Client
Baldwin Publishing
Design Firm
Baldwin Publishing
Designers
Sue Hiltpold,
Suzanne Meyer

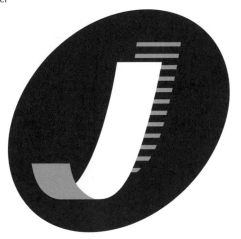

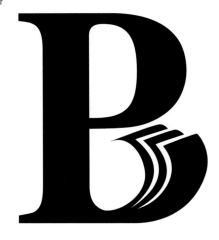

Client
NAVIX
Design Firm
BarrettLaidlawGervais
Designer
David Laidlaw

Client
New Mexico Museum
Natural History
Design Firm
**Rick Johnson &
Company, Inc.**
Designer
Tim McGrath

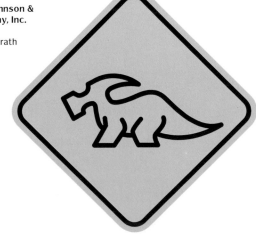

Client
  Daniel Lane, CPA
Design Firm
  The Wecker Group
Designer
  Robert Wecker

DANIEL LANE

Enrolled Agent
Financial and
Tax Planning

"Your Road To Financial Success"

Client
  Johnson County
  Parks & Recreation
Design Firm
  **EAT Advertising
  & Design, Inc.**
Designers
  Patrice Eilts-Jobe,
  John Storey

CELEBRATING 30 YEARS
THEATRE IN THE PARK

Client
  American Heart Association
Design Firm
  EAT Advertising & Design, Inc.
Designer
  DeAnne Kelly

Client
  Avantgo
Design Firm
  1185 Design
Designers
  Dave Prescott,
  Peggy Burke

Client
  The Sandy Paw
  Pet Resort & Park
Design Firm
  **Outta My Mind,
  Visual Communications**
Designer
  Daniel Knol

Client
  Avior
Design Firm
  Connolly & Connolly
Designer
  Dan Collette

261

Client
  Creative Visions
Design Firm
  Creative Visions
Designers
  Cindy Weaver,
  Vern Weaver

Client
  R Squared
Design Firm
  David Day & Associates
Designer
  David Day

Client
  Jerry Schrair & Associates
Design Firm
  Ron Kellum Inc.
Designer
  Ron Kellum

Client
  World Class Customer Satisfaction
Design Firm
  Art Kirsch Graphic Design
Designer
  Art Kirsch

Client
  CornerStone Secure Networks
Design Firm
  The Rakela Company
Designer
  Brian Walima

Client
  Marin County Free Library
Design Firm
  Triad, Inc.
Designer
  Diana Kollanyi

Client
New Mexico Economic Development
Design Firm
Rick Johnson & Company, Inc.
Designer
Tim McGrath

Client
Association of Midwest Museums
Design Firm
Listenberger Design Associates
Designer
Kevin Greek

AMM 1999
Annual Conference
Indianapolis

Client
The Runners
Design Firm
Iconix, Inc.
Designer
Karen Tsang

THE RUNNERS
COURIER SERVICE

Client
Cruise West
Design Firm
Belyea
Designer
Ron Lars Hansen

CruiseWest

Client
Bloomington Offset Printing Inc.
Design Firm
Stan Gellman Graphic Design
Designer
Barry Tilson

VISION
IN PRINT

Client
Merry Land & Investment Company
Design Firm
Crumbley & Alba

MERRITT

Client
   Beckman Coulter, Inc.
Design Firm
   Bright/Point Zero
Designer
   Gary Hinsche

Client
   Rutgers The State
   University of New Jersey
Design Firm
   Office of University
   Publications
Designer
   John Van Cleaf

RUNET 2000

Client
   Tropic Wash, Inc.
Design Firm
   The Baskin Group Inc.
Designers
   Hal Baskin,
   Birgit Kornblum

Client
   Survivair
Design Firm
   RiechesBaird
Designer
   Masa Lau

Client
   Decision Research
Design Firm
   LKF Marketing
Designer
   Sue Severeid

Client
   JM Financial Services
Design Firm
   RKS Design, Inc.
Designers
   Ravi Sawhney,
   Cary Chow,
   Lance Hussey,
   Grace Guy

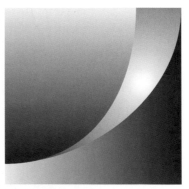

Client
Dr. Susan Love
Design Firm
Hershey Associates
Designer
R. Christine Hershey

Client
Kroll-O'Gara
Design Firm
Three & Associates
Designers
Ted Knapke,
Gordon Cotton

Client
Star Trac
Design Firm
RiechesBaird
Designer
Masa Lau

Client
Pangea Solutions, Inc.
Design Firm
O Design
Designer
Adam Greiss

Client
National Steinbeck Center
Design Firm
Full Steam Marketing & Design
Designer
William L. Owen

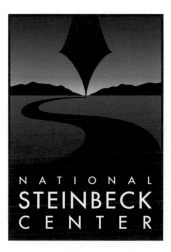

Client
Whitehall Capital
Design Firm
DeMartino Design
Designer
Erick DeMartino

265

Client
University of California, San Diego
(*masthead from a series of icons for
an arts newsletter*)
Design Firm
Tracy Sabin Graphic Design
Designers
Tracy Sabin, Blaize McKinna

Client
Taylor made Golf
(*"e-mail icon" from a series of six
communication icons*)
Design Firm
Laura Coe Design Associates
Designer
Ryoichi Yotsumoto

Client
DataQuick, a division of Axciom
(*two of twelve online property
information icons*)
Design Firm
Laura Coe Design Associates
Designer
Ryoichi Yotsumoto

Client
Road Runner Sports
(*three of eight icons
for a mail order catalog*)
Design Firm
Laura Coe Design Associates
Designer
Ryoichi Yotsumoto

Client
Blue Corn Cafe & Brewery
(*one from a series of seven logos*)
Design Firm
Cisneros Design
Designers
Fred Cisneros, Harry Forehand III
Illustrators
Fred Cisneros,
Beth Evans
Utley

Client
Slavin Schaffer Films
(*one from a series of four logos*)
Design Firm
Susan Hochbaum Design
Designers
Susan Hochbaum,
Steven Guarnaccia

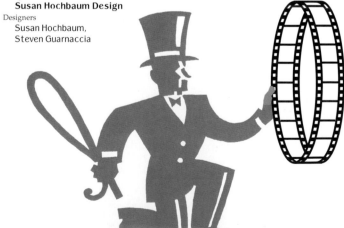

Client
The Jerde Partnership
Design Firm
Selbert Perkins Design Collaborative
Designers
Robin Perkins, John Lutz

Client
Rainbow Programming Holdings
Bravo Profiles
Design Firm
Parham Santana
Creative Director
Bill Snyder (Parham Santana)

Art Director
Emily Pak (Parham Santana)
VP Design Services
Peter Aguanno
(Rainbow Programming Team)
Print Production Manager
Janet Nicosia
(Rainbow Programming Team)

Client
The Los Angeles World Airports
Design Firm
Selbert Perkins Design Collaborative
Designers
Clifford Selbert, Robin Perkins, Rick Simner,
Jamie Diersing, Gemma Lawson

Client
CPI Business Groups
Design Firm
M+P Design Group, Inc.
Designer
Jonathan Westfall

Client
Anacomp
Design Firm
Mires Design, Inc.
Designers
John Ball, Miguel Perez
Art Director
John Ball

Client
Gerber Scientific
Design Firm
Donaldson Makoski Inc.
Designer
Debby Ryan

Client
    Icon Graphics Inc.
Design Firm
    Icon Graphics Inc.

Client
    Yes Strategies Inc.
Design Firm
    Gill Fishman Assoc., Inc.
Designer
    Michael Persons

Client
    PCR
Design Firm
    Dig Design
Designer
    Amy Decker

Client
    ID Biomedical
Design Firm
    Lorenz Advertising & Design
Designer
    Arne Ratermanis

Client
    In the Public Eye
Design Firm
    Fuller Designs, Inc.
Designer
    Doug Fuller

Client
    Houlihan Lokey Howard & Zukin
Design Firm
    Julia Tam Design
Designer
    Julia Tam

268

Client
  Primet Corporation
Design Firm
  Identity Center
Designers
  Wayne Kosterman, Darin Hasley

Client
  Strategics, Inc.
Design Firm
  Jackson Gray
Art Director
  Marti Marsden

Client
  ThermoGenesis
Design Firm
  The Rakela Company
Designer
  Brian Walima

Client
  Fitch Metal Solutions
Design Firm
  Identity Center
Designer
  Wayne Kosterman

Client
  Interior Focus
Design Firm
  Fuller Designs, Inc.
Designer
  Doug Fuller

Client
  Thompson Thrift
Design Firm
  Miller & White Advertising
Designer
  Robert Burch
Creative Director
  Bill White

Client
First Night Pittsburgh
Design Firm
Informatics Studio, Inc.
Designers
Ross Levine, Todd Cavalier

Client
Gator Rock Bits, Inc.
Design Firm
Vividesign Group
Designers
Vividesign Group

First Night® Pittsburgh, Inc.

GATOR

Rock Bits, Inc.

Client
Kansas City Blues & Jazz Festival
Design Firm
Muller + Co.
Designers
John Muller,
Mark Voss

Client
Adventure Publishing
Design Firm
Walsh Associates
Designer
Dan Van Buskirk

Adventure Publishing

Client
Cloudscape, Inc.
Design Firm
Abrams Design Group
Designers
Sander Leech, Zeina Lama

Client
Next Wave Marketing Solutions
Design Firm
Design Manifesto
Designers
Pam Witbeck, Lisa Cumbey

Cloudscape

Client
  Promotional Consultants
Design Firm
  Stan Gellman Graphic Design
Designers
  Barry Tilson,
  Mike Donovan

Client
  Advanta/X-Rail
Design Firm
  Brierton Design
Designers
  Michael Brierton, Martin Cimek

Client
  RKS Design, Inc.
Design Firm
  RKS Design, Inc.
Designer
  Kristin Allen

Client
  Namasté Feng Shui Consulting
Design Firm
  Fuller Designs, Inc.
Designer
  Doug Fuller

Client
  Sunburst Ranch
Design Firm
  The Weller Institute
Designer
  Don Weller

Client
  Tulsa Parks Department
Design Firm
  Walsh Associates
Designer
  Dan Van Buskirk

Client
   Missouri Division of Tourism
Design Firm
   Muller + Co.
Designers
   John Muller, Dave Swearingen

Client
   Smith & Henry
Design Firm
   Kendall Creative Shop
Designer
   Mark K. Platt

Client
   The American Restaurant
Design Firm
   Muller + Co.
Designers
   John Muller, Joann Otto

Client
   Spinergy
Design Firm
   Selbert Perkins Design Collaborative
Designers
   Clifford Selbert, Robin Perkins

Client
   Galileo Foods Company,
   division of Sara Lee
Design Firm
   The Blondo Group
Designer
   Gary Labra

Client
   Louisville Waterfront Development Corp.
Design Firm
   Selbert Perkins Design Collaborative
Designers
   Clifford Selbert, Greg Welch

Client
Delta Beverage Group
Design Firm
Thompson & Company
Designer
Rick Baptist

Client
St. Louis Cardinals
Design Firm
Nehman-Kodner Inc.
Designer
Gary Kodner

DELTA BEVERAGE GROUP

Client
World Blaze
Design Firm
California Design International
Designers
Linda Kelley, Dan Liew

Client
Knowledge Networks
Design Firm
B-Man Design, Inc.
Designer
Barry Brager

WorldBlaze

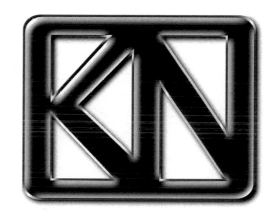

Client
Veda Source
Design Firm
B-Man Design, Inc.
Designer
Tim Theall

Client
Triangle Opera
Design Firm
Peter Taflan Marketing Communications, Inc.
Designer
Janssen Strother

Client
Animal Planet
Design Firm
Fuszion Art + Design
Designers
Anthony Fletcher, Richard Heffner

Client
Horton Plaza
Design Firm
Tracy Sabin Graphic Design
Designers
Tracy Sabin,
Cherilyn Megill

Client
Heirlooms, Inc.
Design Firm
The Wecker Group

Client
Kickapoo Farms
Design Firm
Kendra Power Design & Communication, Inc.
Designer
Larkin Werner

Client
momease
Design Firm
Fuszion Art + Design
Designers
Richard Lee Heffner,
Anthony Fletcher

Client
Mountain Top Heavy Equipment Repair & Service, Inc.
Design Firm
The Wecker Group
Designer
Robert Wecker

Client
   Baldy's Fun Foods
Design Firm
   The Wecker Group
Designer
   Robert Wecker

Client
   Nordstrom
Design Firm
   David Lemley Design
Designers
   David Lemley, Matt Peloza

Client
   Digital Interactive Group
Design Firm
   Hansen Design Company
Designers
   Pat Hansen, Carrie Adams

Client
   The Idea People
Design Firm
   The Wecker Group
Designer
   Robert Wecker

Client
   Missouri Botanical Garden
Design Firm
   Kiku Obata & Company
Designers
   Pam Bliss, Amy Knopf

Client
   Sundance Industries
Design Firm
   Fuszion Art + Design
Designers
   Steve Dreyer,
   Richard Heffner

Client
Navigator Investments
Design Firm
Adkins Balchunas
Designers
Michelle Phaneuf, Matthew Fernberger

Client
The Acme Idea Company
Design Firm
O&J Design, Inc.
Designers
Andrzej J. Olejniczak, Heishin Ra

Client
Codar Ocean Sensors
Design Firm
Gunion Design
Designer
Jefrey Gunion

Client
SRI International
Design Firm
Orak Design
Designer
Coskun Caglayan

Client
Hastings Hot Line Tools & Equipment
Design Firm
LKF Marketing
Designer
Sue Severeid

Client
InnVest Lodging Services Inc.
Design Firm
Crowley Webb + Associates
Designer
Rob Wynne

Client
Bank of America
Design Firm
Enterprise Identity Group
Designers
Will Ayres, Sven Seger, Nina Markarian,
Roy Levitt, Anita Zeppetelli, Bob Wolf

Client
Contech
Design Firm
Insight Design Communications
Designers
Sherrie Holdeman, Tracy Holdeman

Client
Packet Engines
Design Firm
Klundt Hosmer Design
Designer
Darin Klundt

Client
NORTHSTAR Management Co.
Design Firm
CUBE Advertising & Design
Designers
David Chiow, Matt Marino

Client
Burrelle's Information Services
Design Firm
A to Z communications, inc.
Designer
Alan Boarts

Client
Lockheed Martin
Design Firm
James Robie Design Associates
Designer
Karen Nakatani

Client
Thunderbolt Technologies
Design Firm
Jasper & Bridge
Designer
Andy Thorington

Client
Frontenac Bank & Trust
Design Firm
Grizzell & Co
Designer
John H. Grizzell

Client
Strategy Partners
Design Firm
LKF Marketing
Designer
Sue Severeid

Client
Cyberposium '99
Design Firm
Black Bean Studios
Designers
Black Bean Studios

Client
Brian Woolsey
Design Firm
Mires Design, Inc.
Designer, Illustrator
Miguel Perez
Art Director
Scott Mires

Client
Miller Consulting
Design Firm
Gill Fishman Associate, Inc.
Designer
Gill Fishman

?&!

MillerConsulting

Client
Masters of the Web, L.L.C.
Design Firm
Gill Fishman Associates, Inc.
Designer
Alicia Stephenson

Client
Mike 92.7 FM
Design Firm
Insight Design Communications
Designer
Chris Parks

Client
Heaven Group Corp.
Design Firm
Hirano Design Group
Designers
Nobuo Hirano, Ruriko Kinjo

Client
Odyssey
Design Firm
Guarino Graphics
Designer
Jan Guarino

HEAVEN

ODYSSEY

Client
  Opal Computing
Design Firm
  Guarino Graphics
Designer
  Jan Guarino

Client
  R Squared/Vangard
Design Firm
  David Day & Associates
Designer
  David Day

Client
  Parapsychology
Design Firm
  Guarino Graphics
Designer
  Jan Guarino

Client
  Signal Bank
Design Firm
  Karen Skunta & Company
Designers
  Karen L. Hauser, Christopher Oldham,
  Christopher Suster, Karen A. Skunta

Client
  Inland Entertainment
Design Firm
  Mires Design, Inc.
Designers
  José A. Serrano, John Ball, Miguel Perez
Illustrator
  Miguel Perez
Art Director
  José A. Serrano

Client
  Score Asset Management
Design Firm
  Graphic Concepts Group
Designer
  Brian Wilburn

Client
  Human Dimensions in Environmental Systems
  (University of Illinois)
Design Firm
  Clarke Communication Design
Designer
  John V. Clarke

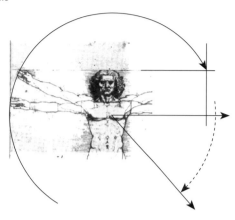

Client
  McClain Forest Products
Design Firm
  Brooks-Jeffrey Marketing

Client
  Behm Printing
Design Firm
  Maddock Douglas, Inc.

Client
  Shadyside Chamber of Commerce
Design Firm
  Robert Meyers Design
Designer
  Robert Meyers

Client
  Moonrise, Inc.
Design Firm
  EAT Advertising & Design, Inc.
Designers
  Patrice Eilts-Jobe, John Storey

INCORPORATED

Client
  Brookdale Homes
Design Firm
  Cornerstone
Designer
  Wilson Fujinaga

Client
Canine Health Foundation
Design Firm
Epstein Design Partners Inc.
Designer
Gina Linehan

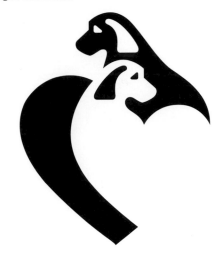

Client
Greyhound Lines
Design Firm
latitude
Designer
Scott Eddy

Client
Drive Communications
Design Firm
Drive Communications
Designer
Michael Graziolo

Client
David Lemley Design
Design Firm
David Lemley Design
Designers
David Lemley, Matt Peloza

Client
The Hearth Shop
Design Firm
The Wecker Group
Designer
Robert Wecker

Client
Omaha Symphony
Design Firm
David Day & Associates
Designer
David Day

Client
  JMAN 5
Design Firm
  Creative Link Studio, Inc.
Designer
  Mark Broderick

Client
  Michael Matthews Productions
Design Firm
  David Day & Associates
Designer
  Joyce Augustinis

Client
  Holocaust Resource Center
Design Firm
  **College Relations Office—
  Keene State College**
Designer
  Christine Justice

Client
  Thor·Lo, Inc.
Design Firm
  Partners & Simons
Designer
  Lori Salmeri

Client
  Children's Cancer Foundation
Design Firm
  Robert Meyers Design
Designer
  Robert Meyers

Client
  Superior Nutrition Corporation
Design Firm
  Martini Studio
Designer
  Shelley Danysh

Client
    Optima, Inc.
Design Firm
    Jack Weiss Associates
Designer
    Jack Weiss

Client
    Fischione Instruments
Design Firm
    A to Z communications, inc.
Designers
    Alan Boarts, Evan Wlmer

Client
    Hilton
Design Firm
    Enterprise Identity Group
Designers
    Gene Grossman, Ryan Paul

Client
    David Lemley Design
Design Firm
    David Lemley Design
Designers
    David Lemley, Matt Peloza

Client
    Mink Vineyard
Design Firm
    The Wecker Group
Designer
    Robert Wecker

Client
    Viant
Design Firm
    California Design International
Designers
    Linda Kelley, Brian Sasville

Client
Merck + Co., Inc.
Design Firm
Madison Design
Designer
Lael Porcelli

Client
Hewlett-Packard
Design Firm
Mortensen Design
Designers
Diana L. Kauzlarich, Gordon Mortensen

Propecia™
(finasteride)

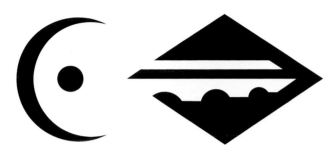

VerSecure

Client
UC Communications
Design Firm
DSI/LA
Designer
Chris Steiner

Client
St. John Design
Design Firm
St. John Design
Designer
Stephen St. John

UC Communications℠

ST JOHN
Design

Client
Wright, Williams & Kelly
Design Firm
The Wecker Group
Designers
Robert Wecker,
Matt Gnibus

Client
Naval Post Graduate School
Design Firm
The Wecker Group
Designer
Robert Wecker

**WRIGHT
WILLIAMS
& KELLY**

**Monterey
Bay
Athletic
Club**

Client
  Monsanto Company
Design Firm
  Stan Gellman Graphic Design
Designers
  Mike Donovan, Barry Tilson

Client
  CSU, Fresno
  Smittcamp Family Honors College
Design Firm
  Shields Design
Designers
  Charles Shields

The Smittcamp Family
HONORS COLLEGE
California State University, Fresno

Client
  Canned Food Alliance
Design Firm
  A to Z communications, inc.
Designer
  Vonnie Hornburg

Client
  Venture Stores
Design Firm
  Phoenix Creative, St. Louis
Designers
  Ed Mantels-Seeker,
  Kathy Wilkinson

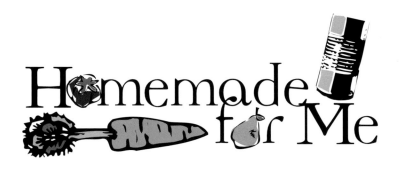

Client
  Thunderbay Stickwear
Design Firm
  Cornerstone
Designer
  Jennifer Kozak

Client
  Janda & Garrington LLC
Design Firm
  Lorenz Advertising & Design
Designer
  Arne Ratermanis

ThunderBay
STiCKWEAR

JANDA &
GARRINGTON
LLC

Client
    Pizza Luna
Design Firm
    Jeff Fisher LogoMotives
Designer
    Jeff Fisher

Client
    Great Pacific Trading Company
Design Firm
    Shields Design
Designer
    Charles Shields
Illustrator
    Doug Hansen

Client
    Dividend Homes, Inc.
Design Firm
    Gauger & Silva
Designers
    Robert Ankers, David Gauger

Client
    Neighbors Manufacturing
Design Firm
    The Weller Institute
Designer
    Don Weller

Client
    Robert Rosenthal
Design Firm
    The Wecker Group
Designer
    Robert Wecker

Client
    Penn Valley Farms
Design Firm
    Design Kitchen Inc.
Designer
    Andy Keene

Client
Alimenterics Inc.
Design Firm
Frank D'Astolfo Design
Designer
Frank D'Astolfo

Client
TTI Systems
Design Firm
David Day & Associates
Designer
David Day

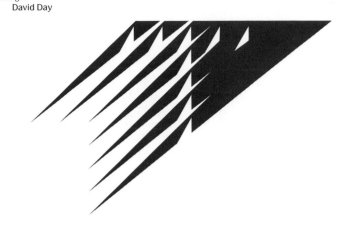

Client
Darien Arts Center
Design Firm
E. Christopher Klumb Associates, Inc.
Designer
Christopher Klumb

Client
Jim Murphy Design, Inc.
Design Firm
Drive Communications
Designer
Michael Graziolo

Client
3COM
Design Firm
Mortensen Design
Designers
Gordon Mortensen,
Wendy Chon

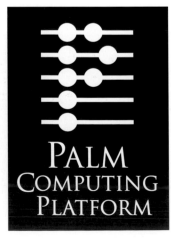

Client
HDS Sales Automation
Design Firm
HDS Marcomm
Designer
Michael McCann

Client
   On-Site Solutions
Design Firm
   Rick Johnson & Company, Inc.
Designer
   Tim McGrath

Client
   Omega Fine Lithographers
Design Firm
   Lane + Lane
Designers
   Brian Lane, Tracey Lane

OMEGA

Client
   Bering Truck Corporation
Design Firm
   ZGraphics, Ltd.
Designers
   Mike Girard, Joe Zeller

Client
   Summit Construction
Design Firm
   Mind's Eye Design
Designer
   Stephen Brown

BERING

Client
   Carleton Corporation
Design Firm
   kor group
Designers
   Karen Dendy, MB Sawyer

Client
   Via Systems
Design Firm
   David Day & Associates
Designer
   David Day

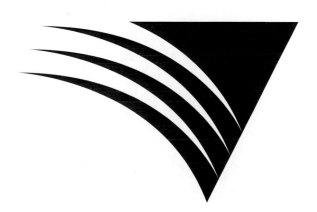

Client
SCLM Software
Design Firm
Taylor Design
Designer
Jennifer Whitaker

Client
ROR Production Studio
Design Firm
Shimokochi/Reeves
Designers
Mamoru Shimokochi, Anne Reeves

Client
Annuncio Software
Design Firm
Focus Design
Designer
Brian Jacobson

Client
Dynegy
Design Firm
Enterprise Identity Group
Designer
Frances Gagliardi

Client
White House Millennium
Design Firm
Carbone Smolan Assoc.
Designers
Justin Peters,
Ken Carbone

Client
National Research Corporation
Design Firm
David Day & Associates
Designer
David Day

Client
Intrigo
Design Firm
RKS Design, Inc.
Designer
Kristin Allen

Client
Chicago Symphony Orchestra
Design Firm
Carbone Smolan Associates
Designers
Claire Taylor,
Justin Peters

Client
Purchase Pro
Design Firm
Creative Dynamics
Designer
Eddie Roberts

Client
Spectrum Photographic
Design Firm
Focus Design
Designer
Brian Jacobson

Client
Jaffe Enterprises
Design Firm
The Visual Group
Designer
Ark Stein

Client
Santa Ana Golf Club,
1999 U.S. Women's Amateur
Public Links Championship
Design Firm
Rick Johnson & Company, Inc.
Designer
Tim McGrath
Art Director
Rick Gutierrez

Client
American Escrow & Closing Company
Design Firm
Crosby Associates Inc.
Designers
Bart Crosby, Carl Wohlt

Client
TerraMetrics, Inc.
Design Firm
Design Room
Designer
Chad Gordon

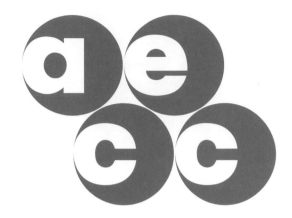

Client
Nextlevel Systems, Inc.
Design Firm
Crosby Associates Inc.
Designer
Bart Crosby

Client
Rosewood Hotels & Resorts
Design Firm
VWA Group
Designer
Ashley Barron

NEXT LEVEL

PALM COURT

Client
LKF Marketing
Design Firm
LKF Marketing
Designer
Sue Severeid

Client
MeriStar Hotels & Resorts, Inc.
Design Firm
Crosby Associates Inc.
Designer
Bart Crosby

LKF *Marketing* !

MERISTAR

Client
Philip Salaverry Photography
Design Firm
Mitten Design
Designers
Marianne Mitten,
David Kepner

Client
Renaissance Dental Management
Design Firm
HC Creative Communications
Designers
Howard Clare, Chuck Sundin

Client
The Wharton School
Design Firm
Joel Katz Design Associates

Client
Envision Creative
Design Firm
Envision Creative
Designer
Bryan Cooper

Client
J. Patrick Moore & Partners/Hanchi Corp.
Design Firm
Hedstrom/Blessing
Designer
Pam Goebel

Client
Phoenix Partners
Design Firm
Straightline International
Designer
Jane Bocker

293

Client
   Blue Corn Cafe
Design Firm
   Cisneros Design
Designer
   Fred Cisneros

BLUE CORN
CAFE & BREWERY
tortillas, tequila y cerveza

Santa Fe, New Mexico

Client
   USC
Design Firm
   The Visual Group
Designer
   Ark Stein

Client
   Level 3 Communications
Design Firm
   Webster Design Associates
Designers
   Sean Heisler, Dave Webster

suggestionBOX

Client
   Creative Dynamics Inc.
Design Firm
   Creative Dynamics Inc.
Designers
   Dawn Teagarden, Eddie Roberts

CREATIVE DYNAMICS INC

Client
   Personify
Design Firm
   Hornall Anderson Design Works
Designers
   Jack Anderson, Debra McCloskey, Holly Finlayson

Client
   Northwest Vista College
Design Firm
   DiBaggio Design
Designers
   Brad DiBaggio,
   John Keoni Viriyapunt

NORTHWEST
VISTA
COLLEGE

Client
  Mississippi Space Commerce Initiative
Design Firm
  NewIDEAS, Inc.
Designer
  Patty O. Seger

MISSISSIPPI
S P A C E
COMMERCE
INITIATIVE

Client
  National Policy & Resource Center
  for Women & Aging
Design Firm
  Susan Bercu
  Design Studio
Designer
  Susan Bercu

WOMEN & AGING

Client
  Pittsburgh Symphony Orchestra
Design Firm
  Kendra Power Design &
  Communication, Inc.
Designer
  Kathy Kendra

soundbytes
MORE HERE THAN MEETS THE EAR

Client
  Deloitte & Touche
Design Firm
  Orak Design
Designer
  Tuncel Goklepinar

1 9 9 8

VISION IN

MANUFACTURING

Client
  Irideon
Design Firm
  latitude
Designer
  Rob Johnson

IRIDEON

Client
  Karlo the Magician
Design Firm
  Maremar, Inc.
Designer
  Marina Rivón

KARLO

Client
Avrin Public Relations Group
Design Firm
X Design Company
Designer
Alex
Valderrama

Client
Opinion Research
Design Firm
Paganucci Design
Designers
Bob Paganucci, Frank Paganucci

Client
DuClaw Restaurant & Brewing Co.
Design Firm
Gr8
Designer
Alain Bolduc

Client
Online Communications
Design Firm
Gr8
Designer
Lisa Wurfl-Roeca

Client
Enterworks
Design Firm
Elliott Van Deutsch
Designers
Blake Stenning, Marc Foelsch

Client
Photo Communications
Design Firm
Gr8
Designers
Alicia Leaf, Morton Jackson, Lisa Wurfl-Roeca

Client
University of Denver
Design Firm
North Charles Street Design Organization
Art Director
Mark Shippe
Creative Director
Bernice A. Thieblot

Client
IconixGroup
Design Firm
IconixGroup
Designers
John Cabot Lodge, Sid Barcelona, Claire Cesna

Client
The National Conference for Community and Justice
Design Firm
Malcolm Grear Designers

Client
One 3 Restaurant
Design Firm
Di Vision Studio
Designer
Cristiana Neri

Client
Custom Business Systems, Inc.
Design Firm
Funk & Associates
Designer
Christopher Berner

Client
Velocity Grill
Design Firm
Franek Design Associates, Inc.
Designers
David Franek, Amy Puglisi

Client
Sunstar, Inc.
Design Firm
Desgrippes Gobé
Designer
Susan Berson

Client
JWA Associates
Design Firm
Visual Marketing Associates
Designer
Jason Selke

Client
  T-Bird Aviation
Design Firm
  Visual Marketing Associates
Designer
  Tracy Meiners

Client
  Falcon Plastics, Inc.
Design Firm
  Kendra Power Design & Communication, Inc.
Designer
  Matthew Wensel

Client
  Snowmass Club
Design Firm
  Schwener Design Group
Designers
  Diane Schwener,
  Cynthia Brown Bringas

Client
  WagDog
Design Firm
  Jeffrey Leder Inc.
Designer
  Carlos Tejeda

Client
  Moffat County, Colorado
Design Firm
  Pollman Marketing Arts, Inc.
Designers
  Jennifer Pollman, Leslie Blanton

Client
  Human Pheromone Sciences, Inc.
Design Firm
  Louisa Sugar Design
Designers
  Louisa Sugar,
  Albert Treskin

Client
Riggs Bank
Design Firm
ICONIXGROUP
Designers
John Cabot Lodge, Roo Johnson

Client
Young Presidents' Organization
Design Firm
Swieter Design U.S.
Designer
Mark Ford

Client
Spider Securities
Design Firm
Visual Asylum
Designers
Amy Jo Levine, MaeLin Levine, Charles Glaubitz

Client
Sirgany Enterprises
Design Firm
Pavlik Design Team
Designer
Renee Farrugia

Client
Rocky Mountain Bail Bonds
Design Firm
The Weller Institute
Designer
Don Weller

Client
Caffe Focaccia
Design Firm
The Visual Group
Designer
Ark Stein

Client
Scarola Associates
Design Firm
Design Kitchen Inc.
Designer
Jamie Anderson

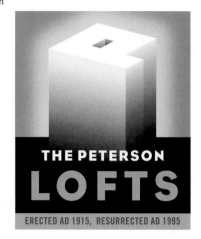

Client
CoreSource, Inc.
Design Firm
Crosby Associates Inc.
Designers
Bart Crosby, Carl Wohlt

Client
Rich-Mar Corporation
Design Firm
Tim Girvin Design, Inc.
Designer
Michele Carter

Client
Champion International Corporation
Design Firm
Crosby Associates, Inc.
Designer
Bart Crosby

Client
Hewitt Associates LLC
Design Firm
Crosby Associates Inc.
Designer
Bart Crosby

Client
Deep Cool Nightclub
Design Firm
Phoenix Creative, St. Louis
Designer
Steve Wienke

Client
    Hope Youth Center
Design Firm
    Dotzler Creative Arts
Designers
    Dotzler Creative Arts

Client
    Lycos
Design Firm
    Wallace/Church
Designers
    Stan Church, Craig Swanson

Client
    Pepsico Restaurants International
Design Firm
    Design Continuum Inc
Designer
    Jane Hathaway

Client
    Design Continuum Inc
Design Firm
    Design Continuum Inc
Designers
    Michelle Tsay, Richard Davia, Claire Bowen

Client
    Great Expectations
Design Firm
    The Wecker Group
Designer
    Robert Wecker

Client
    self promotion
Design Firm
    The Imagination Company
Designers
    Steve Frigard, Mark Connelly

Client
Sirgany Enterprises
Design Firm
Pavlik Design Team
Designer
Renee Farrugia

Client
Strings Incorporated
Design Firm
Perlman Company
Designer
Robert Perlman

Client
Isabel Parlett
Design Firm
Quinne Design Associates
Designer
Quinne Fokes

Client
OSEL Incorporated
Design Firm
Focus Design
Designer
Brian Jacobson

ÖSEL

Client
MLSPA
Design Firm
Grafik Communications
Designers
David Collins, Judy Kirpich

Client
Sinogen
Design Firm
Artemis Creative, Inc.
Designers
Wes Aoki, Gary Nusinow

SINO(GEN

Client
Lutheran Brotherhood
Design Firm
Yamamoto Moss
Designer
Alan Tse

Client
Evocative, Inc.
Design Firm
Tsuchiya Sloneker Communications
Designer
Douglas Ridgway

The **Fisher's** Net

evocative

Client
Tuesday's Child
Design Firm
Design Kitchen Inc.
Designer
Tracy Rodgers

Client
MarketSoft Corporation
Design Firm
Stewart Monderer Design, Inc.
Designer
Stewart Monderer

Tuesday's Child

MarketSoft™

Client
Neworld, Entertainment International
Design Firm
Design Edge

Client
Chase Global Mutual Funds
Design Firm
Hanson Associates, Inc.
Designer
Christy Beck

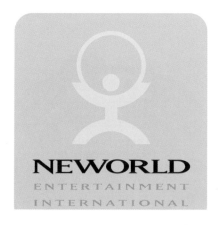

NEWORLD
ENTERTAINMENT
INTERNATIONAL

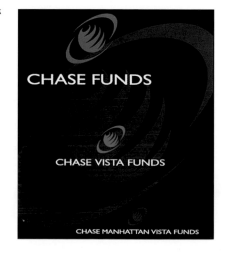

CHASE FUNDS

CHASE VISTA FUNDS

CHASE MANHATTAN VISTA FUNDS

Client
  Noblestar
Design Firm
  IconixGroup
Designers
  John Cabot Lodge, Robert C. Coleman, David Neal Wiseman

Client
  Aullwood Audubon & Farm
Design Firm
  Visual Marketing Associates
Designer
  Michael Butts

Client
  Marriott Hotels, Resorts and Suites
Design Firm
  Bailey Design Group, Inc.
Designers
  Steve Perry, Wendy Seldomridge

Client
  Joy Tree
Design Firm
  neo design
Designer
  Kristi
  Antonneau

Client
  Asilomar Conference Center
Design Firm
  Full Steam Marketing & Design
Designer
  Darryl Zimmerman, Peter Hester

Client
  Green Field Paper Company
Design Firm
  Mires Design
Designers
  José A. Serrano, Miguel Perez
Illustrator
  Tracy Sabin
Art Director
  José A. Serrano

Client
Pasta Pomodoro
Design Firm
Cisneros Design
Designer
Eric Griego

Client
Ergo Health Systems
Design Firm
WATCH! Graphic Design
Designer
Bruno Watel

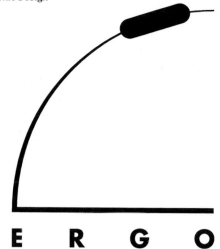

Client
Parkworks Cleveland
Design Firm
Epstein Design Partners Inc.
Designers
Anne Toomey,
Gina Linehan

Client
Wellness Business Works, Ltd.
Design Firm
Murrie Lienhart Rysner
Designer
Linda Voll

Client
Optima, Inc.
Design Firm
Jack Weiss Associates
Designer
Jack Weiss

Client
Flowers & Gifts.com
Design Firm
Yamamoto Moss
Designer
Brian Adducci

Client
Dept. of City Planning, Pittsburgh
Design Firm
Agnew Moyer Smith Inc.
Designers
Norm Goldberg,
John Sotirakis,
Bob Whitehouse

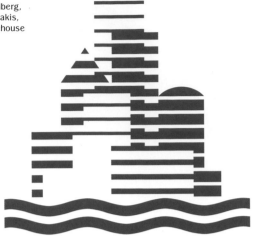

Client
Brother International
Design Firm
Design Edge

Client
MLR
Design Firm
Murrie Lienhart Rysner
Designer
Jim Lienhart

Client
Linda Gusick
Design Firm
Murrie Lienhart Rysner
Designer
Jim Lienhart

Client
GLS Consulting
Design Firm
Waterman Design
Designer
Priscilla White Sturges

Client
The Fine Line
Design Firm
Murrie Lienhart Rysner
Designer
Linda Voll

Client
Altec Lansing Technologies
Design Firm
Ronald Emmerling Design, Inc.
Designer
Ronald Emmerling

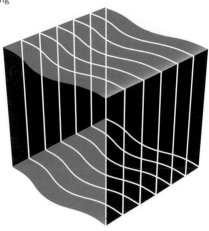

Client
Cape Cod Healthcare
Design Firm
Malcolm Grear Designers

Client
Intelligent Biocides
Design Firm
Phoenix Creative, St. Louis
Designer
Ed Mantels-Seeker

INTELLIGENT BIOCIDES

Client
MLR
Design Firm
Murrie Lienhart Rysner
Designer
Jim Lienhart

Client
Edison Brothers Stores
Design Firm
Phoenix Creative, St. Louis
Designer
Jenny Anderson

Client
Lighthouse Holdings, Inc.
Design Firm
Kendra Power Design & Communication, Inc.
Designer
Larkin Werner

LIGHTHOUSE HOLDINGS

Client
HDS Channel Marketing
Design Firm
HDS Marcomm
Designer
Michael McCann

Channel One
Reseller Program

Client
General Magic
Design Firm
Hornall Anderson Design Works
Designers
Jack Anderson, Jana Nishi,
Larry Anderson,
Mike Brugman,
Mary Chin Hutchison

Client
Environmental Protection Agency
Design Firm
Levine and Associates
Designer
Andrew Criss

Client
Portage Financial Management
Design Firm
WATCH! Graphic Design
Designer
Bruno Watel

Environmental
Accounting
Project

PORTAGE

Client
Serrano Interiors
Design Firm
Swieter Design U.S.
Designer
Mark Ford

Client
Conversā
Design Firm
Hornall Anderson Design Works
Designers
Jack Anderson, Kathy Saito, Alan Copeland

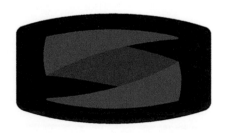

conversā

Client
Fritz!
Design Firm
Corey McPherson Nash
Designers
Kristin Reid, Paddy McCobb

Client
Rosewood Hotels & Resorts
Design Firm
VWA Group
Designer
Ashley Barron

Client
General Magic
Design Firm
Hornall Anderson Design Works
Designers
Jack Anderson, Jana Nishi,
Mary Chin Hutchison,
Larry Anderson,
Mike Brugman

Client
Ingear Corporation
Design Firm
Visual Marketing Associates
Designer
Joshua Schwochow

Client
Associated Construction
Design Firm
Klundt Hosmer Design
Designers
Darin Klundt, Amy Gunter

Client
Perlman Company
Design Firm
Perlman Company
Designer
Robert Perlman

Client
TriMech
Design Firm
Fuller Designs, Inc.
Designer
Laura Beirne

Client
Juniper Communications
Design Firm
Pollman Marketing Arts, Inc.
Designer
Jennifer Pollman

TRIMECH
SOLUTIONS

Client
S A USA
Design Firm
FRCH Design Worldwide (New York)
Designer
Christina Antonopoulos

Client
Aids Project Rhode Island
Design Firm
Malcolm Grear Designers

Client
The Atticus Group
Design Firm
Rousso + Associates
Designer
Steve Rousso

Client
McDermott Planning & Design
Design Firm
X Design Company
Designer
Alex Valderrama

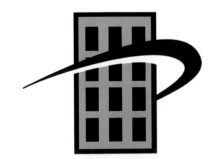

ATTICUS

Client
Jay Cosso
Design Firm
X Design Company
Designer
Alex
Valderrama

Client
Transcore
Design Firm
Bailey Design Group, Inc.
Designer
Laura Markley

Client
Van Der Bosch
Design Firm
WATCH! Graphic Design
Designer
Bruno Watel

Client
Jagtiani + Associates
Design Firm
Fuller Designs, Inc.
Designer
Doug Fuller

Jagtiani+Associates
Protecting your ideas

Client
Mount Everest Project
Design Firm
Maremar, Inc.
Designers
Marina Rivón

Client
Tobey + Davis Architects
Design Firm
Fuller Designs, Inc.
Designers
Doug Fuller, Aaron Taylor

T O B E Y + D A V I S

Client
The Richard E. Jacobs Group
Design Firm
Herip Associates
Designers
Walter Herip, John Menter

The Richard E. Jacobs Group

Client
Colorado's Ocean Journey
Design Firm
Rassman Design
Designers
John Rassman,
Amy Rassman,
Lyn D'Amato,
Vicki Freeman,
Gwyn Browning

OCEAN JOURNEY℠
PRESENTED BY US WEST

Client
Dimension Enterprises
Design Firm
Gr8
Designers
Rob Rhinehart, Morton Jackson

DIMENSION
ENTERPRISES

Client
Wolfram Research, Inc.
Design Firm
Wolfram Research, Inc.
Designer
John Bonadies

PUBLICON™

Client
Fortner Software
Design Firm
Gr8
Designer
Rob Rhinehart

fortner
software

Client
Rep File, Inc.
Design Firm
X Design Company
Designer
Alex Valderrama

Client
Sun International
Design Firm
David Carter Design Associates
Designer
Tien Pham
Creative Director
Lori B. Wilson

Client
Lewis Energy Group
Design Firm
DiBaggio Design
Designer
Brad DiBaggio

Olmos Drilling, L.L.C.

Client
  Fortress Technologies, Inc.
Design Firm
  Roman Design
Designer
  Lisa Romanowski

Client
  Mission Studios
Design Firm
  Conflux Design
Designer
  Greg Fedorev

Client
  Paradysz Matera Company
Design Firm
  Division Studio
Designer
  Cristiana Neri

Client
  Jaggo Sports
Design Firm
  Swieter Design U.S.
Designer
  Mark Ford

Client
  SuperSonic BOOM
Design Firm
  Gr8
Designer
  Lisa Wurfl-Roeca

Client
  Hammerquist & Halverson
Design Firm
  Hornall Anderson Design Works
Designers
  Jack Anderson,
  Mike Calkins

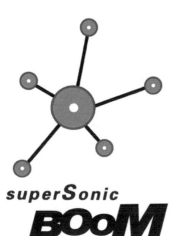

Client
Consentino's Restaurants
Design Firm
Design Kitchen Inc.
Designer
Jamie Anderson

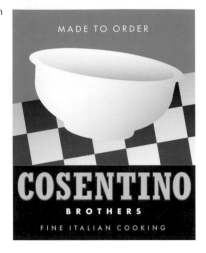

Client
Lee Lime Corp
Design Firm
Handler Design Group
Designer
Bruce Handler,
John Ryan

Client
Taylor Guitars
Design Firm
Tracy Sabin Graphic Design
Designers
Tracy Sabin, Rita Hoffman

Client
The Ridge Resort
Design Firm
The Flowers Group
Designers
Tracy Sabin, Cory Sheehan

Client
Farwest Airlines
Design Firm
Morgan & Co.
Designer
David Morgan
Illustrator
Roland Dahlquist

Client
Equinox
Design Firm
Wechsler Ross & Partners Inc.
Senior Designer
Amber de Janosi
Design Director
Stephen Visconti

Design Firm
Lewis Design
Designers
Tracy Sabin, June Lewis

Client
Borders, Inc./
National Association of Recording Merchandisers
Design Firm
Phoenix Creative, St. Louis
Designer
Deborah
Finkelstein

Client
Zehnder's Marketplace
Design Firm
JGA, Inc.
(Jon Greenberg & Assoc)
Designer
Brian Eastman

Client
Stackwoods Restaurant
Design Firm
Marve Cooper Design
Designers
Tracy Sabin,
Doug Hardenburgh

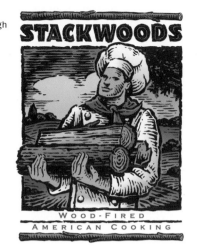

Client
Unocal Corporation
Design Firm
Douglas Joseph Partners
Designer
Koji Takei

Client
Anheuser-Busch Specialty Brewing
Design Firm
Phoenix Creative, St. Louis
Designer
Kathy Wilkinson

315

Index

319